To Mom:

on mother's day - 1961 May 14th

Lawrence, Veda
Dean & Arlene

TO MY SON

To My Son

FAITH AT OUR HOUSE

Dale Evans Rogers

FLEMING H. REVELL COMPANY

Westwood, New Jersey

Library of Congress Catalog Card Number: 57-6856

Printed in the United States of America

1.6

To

my beloved mother and son,

without whom

this book might never have been written.

May their example of unswerving faith

in the Lord Jesus Christ

be honored

throughout my earthly pilgrimage.

These are letters, written out of my heart, to my son Tom.

They are printed here, not that I might boast, but that I might share the fellowship of other mothers as concerned as I am with the unfolding of a lively faith in their children. . . .

. . . and that I might share with them the problems we have met and the answers we have found in working out a faith at our house. . . .

Dale Evans Rogers

TO MY SON

Dear Tom

There is so much I want to tell you that I am afraid this is going to be a very long letter! Life is hectic these days and there never seems to be enough time to say all the things I have in my heart for you.

I think you are a pretty wonderful boy. It isn't that I am just prejudiced because you are my son; it's because you are such a good Christian. I imagine most mothers think their sons are the finest in the world and I am no exception! But instead of my boasting, "Look at the fine boy I raised!", I should say, "Look at the fine boy who raised me!" A strange statement? It is true, because you raised me to life the night you led me, your own mother, to my Lord and Saviour, Jesus Christ.

From the moment the nurse in the hospital at Memphis, Tennessee, placed you, my first born, in my arms, you have blessed my life. You were a quiet little boy, with enormous brown eyes. I thought you were almost too pretty to be a boy. You know Dick West, the cowboy actor who plays "Buffalo Bill, Jr." on television? Well, his name was Dickie Jones when he was a little boy starting in pictures. I cut his picture out of a magazine one day, because you two little tykes looked enough alike to be twins. Never did I dream that one day you would both be in Hollywood—that he would be a young cowboy star who attended the Hollywood Christian Group, and that you would be teaching music in Los Angeles public schools and directing a choir at a Pasadena church—and you know, Tom, I think you both did well!

You sang before you talked. I can still see you sitting on the floor in Mom's apartment in Memphis, Tennessee, playing with your blocks as you hummed, "They Cut Down the Old Pine Tree." Mom and I thought you were never going to talk—but how you loved music! I was very busy those days, trying to "establish" myself, to get security for you and me. Isn't it too bad I didn't know that security was there all the time in the person of our Lord and Saviour, Jesus Christ? You always loved Christ and the church, Tom. You reminded me of Samuel in the Bible, because even when you were a little lad it seemed you wanted to say, "Here am I, Lord," because you answered his call very early in life—and sincerely.

How wonderful the Lord was to send you to me. Yours was a turbulent life. After your father and I parted, there were years of struggling to "get ahead" and always hoping I would find a partner who would be a good father for you. Remarriage for me was a failure, because I was not a Christian. This I believe with all my heart. I get so many letters from parents and children, asking advice on this particular problem. The road of a stepparent and stepchild is indeed a rocky one. I have found the only chance for happiness in situations like these is for the parents both to be Christian, to put the Lord at the head of the house, and to remember that if we truly belong to Him, we live like brothers and sisters in Him. This is something I know from experience.

Roy and I and all the children here wouldn't have lasted a year together if the Lord hadn't graciously decided to make Himself known to me, and then to Roy. Rather, I should say, we asked Him to make Himself known to us and to come into our lives and help us—and He did. Ours would have been just another "Hollywood marriage on the rocks." The sea has been very rough at times, son, but the Captain of our souls has always intervened at the right time and righted our craft. Jesus is so wonderful that I shall never be able to say enough for Him and what He has done for me and mine. He is so true to His promises—and I believe He expects the same of us. This is something I have thought of so many times since little Robin left us.

Do you remember the time in Louisville, Kentucky, when you were five that I came home from a broadcast to find you horribly nauseated, with aching neck and legs? It happened at the time of the bad infantile paralysis epidemic there. What a tortured hour I spent, waiting at the hospital, as they tapped your spine to determine your case. I prayed so hard the test would be negative, and told the Lord if He would protect you from this disease I would put Him first the rest of my life. What a blessed relief to have the doctor say "negative"! How different things might have been for you and me—and everyone else concerned—if I had only kept my promise.

I am sad to say I forgot the promise. But the Lord did not forget. Many years later I was to be praying for the healing of my second child—little Robin. This time I really was desperate, because she came into the world handicapped. I told Him if He would touch her little mind and body and cause her to be normal, I would spend the rest of my life telling people what He had done. He must have known I wouldn't have the courage to keep my end of such a bargain, for fear some people would doubt that Robin was really healed and would stare at her and whisper about her. I believe He knew that fear for the welfare of my beloved little angel would prevent me from declaring the miracle He had wrought—and so He took her mercifully Home, where she would be forever at peace. Then He whispered to my soul, "All right, she is healed forever, and in a place where no one will be critically curious; now you go tell my children where they can find the answer to their problems!"

I have just been reading the twelfth chapter of Ecclesiastes: "Remember now thy Creator in the days of thy youth, while the evil days come not, nor the years draw nigh, when thou shalt say, I have no pleasure in them. . . ." How wise, indeed, is the child who places his love and trust in the Lord Jesus Christ at an early age, talks with Him daily by prayer and by the reading of His Word, the Holy Bible. Your life and mine, Tom, might have been forever blighted had you not wholeheartedly given yourself to the Lord at the age of ten, and stayed with Him through all those bewildering years that followed. I, too, made a declaration of faith in Jesus Christ when I was ten, but not with my whole heart. There's a great difference, and *what* a difference it makes in the life of the individual! You asked Him to be your Saviour and Master; I only asked Him to be my Saviour. I was like a child unable to swim, asking his parent to stand on the shore and watch as he ventured out into the deep water—and if he should start to sink, to save him! The child needs the parent with him in the water, to hold him up if he steps over his head. Far better that way, than nearly to drown before he calls for help! The point is that we are always children in God's eyes, and we need God's guidance all the way through life. Our own wisdom is never sufficient to meet the trials that confront us.

This morning, while getting my hair curled for the television series, Mildred, our hairdresser, and I were discussing Eugenia Price's book *Never a Dull Moment*, and I told her that was to be one of your birthday gifts, since Genie so brilliantly and forthrightly challenges our youth to follow a Lord who was and is and always will be MAN and GOD; a Lord and Saviour who was not afraid to resist evil. Young people have long had the mistaken idea that Christ and His followers were weak characters who "took it on the chin" for a lost cause. If only they could realize that He is the greatest hero of all and that to follow Him means to live the most challenging, stimulating, exciting and rewarding life. To follow Him means to face the most crucial tests of life bravely, with full assurance of ultimate victory in Him.

I had a remarkable experience with a teen-ager friend not long ago. He has a keen mind and a discerning one. He is a boy who rationalizes and wants an answer to everything. He was curious about my faith, and I believe wanted to know what "made me tick." He said that he had accepted Christ by faith at a summer retreat camp, and that he had a wonderful spiritual experience there; he then decided to test our Lord to see if He would "come through" for him. At the time he needed a job very badly, and there were four or five good jobs open. He applied for one and did not get it. He lost heart, and thought the Lord had let him down. And people that he thought were Christians disappointed him by their actions —and their "Sunday religion." Disgusted, he gradually drifted away from the Lord, and had ended up a bewildered and mixed-up boy.

We had a wonderful talk, and it helped me to get an insight into one teen-ager's spiritual problems. He seemed to want the "two-and-two-make-four" answers to faith, and to work it like arithmetic. This attitude I find very prevalent today. Jesus said, "Except ye . . . become as little children, ye shall not enter into the kingdom of heaven." A baby does not demand the answer as to how his bottle warmer works; he just enjoys the warm milk it produces! I told him that just because he doubted the validity of God's promises did not mean that God is not true to His promises; that he simply had not learned to "wait upon God." When we try to "put God on the spot," we are guilty of tempting Him as Satan tempted Jesus in the desert to command the stones to become bread. I gave him my testimony and told him how the

Lord had worked in my life since I surrendered it to Him. I told him how He had allowed me to face some very hard moments, but that I had never doubted His power to accomplish His purpose for my life, and therefore He gave me understanding in His own time: He made me see that we are not to question *when* the answer will come. God's answers are very often "No," because He knows that the request is for something that will retard our spiritual growth. I sent this boy Eugenia Price's *Never a Dull Moment* this Christmas—and yesterday received my reward. He wrote me: "Remember the book you gave me? Well, I took it on a trip, and although I didn't have much time to read, the time I did spend on it taught me something. I can't exactly put my finger on it, but when I got home I read it again, as I would a schoolbook, not just another novel —and I've been thinking. . . . I once thought (and I still do, to some extent) that a person's mind was his greatest enemy, but I have learned that it can also be a person's greatest friend. It all depends on how he uses it. Thinking back over the talks we have had and the books I have read, I believe I have found the key to my poor outlook on religion. I have always tried to "live on my own two feet"; if I do the right thing, fine; if I do the wrong thing, I try not to give an *excuse*. I can't put enough into that word 'excuse,' because I think an excuse is the cheapest thing under the sun; it takes a man to say 'I'm sorry, I was wrong!' I think that's been my trouble. I've been making excuses for myself instead of accepting the challenge of a Christian life, and I am still a little hesitant about accepting it. I guess I'm confused about the whole thing, but I do want to thank you for what you have done for me, and I hope you don't think me silly but I can talk to you because you have been around and you call a spade a spade. You don't try to bluff or exaggerate an idea or a set of circumstances. I am glad to call you my friend. If you ever run across another person like myself (God forbid), please don't hesitate to use this letter in your conversion of him."

Of course, Tom, *I* did not convert this boy. The Holy Spirit alone can do that—and the Lord, alone, knows if this boy is converted, or really "turned around." The point is that children are *direct* in their seeking today—and they want us to be honest about our own failings and tell them the truth about what God has to offer as against the offerings of the world. They are disappointed in Christianity when they are promised that Christ is a glorified Santa Claus, and they are disappointed in Him if their every whim is not granted. Our whole world has become so materialistic that our children can only think in terms of "things"—and this is frustrating.

Our children need to see Christ in their parents. They need to see Christian assurance and serenity in us in time of trouble and sorrow. They need to see us seeking God's will for our lives, rather than forever searching for worldly pleasure. In short, *they are mainly what they see in their parents.* This may be strong talk, Tom, but I believe it. The only reason you were different as a teenager was because you walked close to the Lord and depended on Him instead of on me. How I thank Him for making Himself known to you and surrounding you with His peace and assurance that He would answer your prayers in my behalf!

Last Sunday afternoon was one of the mountain peaks of my spiritual experience. To see you standing so straight and tall, directing that wonderful choir in the incomparable Handel's *Messiah* was a delight to my soul. When you were eleven, I bought you a flute in Chicago and you started taking lessons. Caesar Petrillo, the orchestra leader at CBS in Chicago, where I was employed as staff singer, told me that real, honest-to-goodness "flautists" (flute players) were scarce, and if you were really good you would earn a fine living in the music field. When we first moved to Los Angeles it seemed you were practicing all day, every day! A prominent orchestra leader heard you play one day and told me you had great promise. I started to dream of the day I would see you conducting a concert in the Hollywood Bowl, and hear your clear flute passages here and there in motion picture musical scores. Knowing a few people in the entertainment industry, I began figuring on various "contacts" to get you launched on your musical career. Imagine my horrified surprise when you looked me kindly but squarely in the eye and said, "I appreciate your wanting to help me get started, but I have chosen another career: I want to spend my life reaching boys and girls for God through music. I am going to teach music, good music that will point them toward God."

Being virtually blind of Spirit at that time, your announcement floored me. My castle crumbled. . . . Little did I realize then that the cornerstone for a heavenly mansion had just been laid, for when the celestial strains of Handel's *Messiah* rose from your flowing fingers and swelled into the "Hallelujah Chorus," I thanked God that you had chosen "the better part." Alone, driving home through a downpour, I thought of many things—of an increasing juvenile delinquency; of the rapidly rising divorce rate; of youthful dope addiction. I pondered the possibility of writing a book my publishers had requested on "Religion in the Home," and I decided that I must share my thoughts on this matter with you. Hence, this long, long letter. . . .

There are many disturbing elements in the lives of our young people today, Tom. For instance, there are those who seek to destroy, by any means they can, the validity of the Christian witness. One way is to abuse our precious freedom of speech through the press, by printing unfavorable items about public figures who profess Christ as Saviour. Poor, benighted souls; they need prayer, for they do not realize that they are the tools of Satan who is the adversary of men. I believe Satan would like to corrupt the moral integrity of American youth, and that he delights in destroying the illusions of children by printing ugly stories about their favorite heroes. Some of the stories are no doubt true—and some are pathetically false. Little does he care that the brightness of a childhood dream is tarnished. The children are the ones hurt by these attacks, because adults understand that no one is perfect.

The true Christian loves his enemies, but hates the evil. Therefore he prays for his attackers, that God will give them understanding and open the eyes of their souls, for they are, in reality, spiritually blind and to be pitied. How wonderful to be a Christian and know beyond the shadow of a doubt that God has cleansed or will cleanse us of sin by the shed blood of Jesus Christ, and through the spiritual bathing of His Holy Spirit. We need not fear what man can do—for if God be for us, who can be against us? St. Paul tells us that nothing can separate us from the love of Christ—and this is all that matters. The Bible says that man judges by outward appearances but God judges the heart.

It is hard to be a Christian, Tom, but glorious; and it is the most exciting venture of life—because Christ *is* life! You know the saying about airplane pilots reaching the "point of no return" on a trip? Son, I have passed the point of no return on my Christian pilgrimage. I am sure the way henceforth will be steep and perilous, but my Guide is dependable and He promises the summit, even though we may be gasping when we reach there. Jesus is the Pearl of Great Price, and in order to possess Him eternally, it may be necessary to forfeit dearly. But let me ask you, what else is there? St. Paul says "Having done all, stand!" Lord, help me to stand straight and unflinching. You have given and suffered so much for us. Why should we expect a rosy and smooth path?

Lovingly yours,
Mother.

Dear Tom

There are so many people who cannot understand why Christians have to suffer. It is difficult for them to believe that one is made better by suffering, and that a true Christian counts it a privilege to sacrifice or suffer for Jesus' sake. How I praise God for some shining examples He has shown me!

There was the day in Encino, when you and Barbara took little Mindy, your first born, to the pediatrician for a routine check up. You were staying with us during your summer vacation from teaching school in Yreka, and working on your Master's degree at U.S.C. Mom Smith was also visiting us. Little Robin was doing pretty well at the time. Your Mindy was a darling, lively baby girl of six months, and seemed the picture of health. I remember that I was shampooing my hair when Mom walked in and quietly but tensely said, "Mindy is going to have to go into a crippled children's hospital—she is crippled!"

I was too stunned to speak for a moment. Then, before

I could stop myself, I cried with protest, "It isn't fair! What have Tom and Barbara ever done to deserve this? They have been dedicated Christians since they were children! I can't understand it, Mom; I just can't take it!" Mom looked at me kindly but sternly, and (bless her heart) she said, "Straighten yourself up, and go comfort those kids. They haven't complained once, and are taking it like good soldiers. You ought to be ashamed to talk like that!" From that one speech of your grandmother's I knew what a wonderful influence she had been in your life, Tom—and how grateful I would forever be to my Mom for the Christian training she gave you in your early years. Humbled to the core, I apologized to Mom and to God for my outburst. I had never questioned God or complained about Robin's condition because she had arrived that way, and He had given me the grace to accept it and to entrust her to His care. But to hear that lovable, bouncing little Mindy was minus one hip socket and that there was a possibility that she might not walk normally was a terrific shock to me. I braced myself and went in to the living room to talk to you. You were very white, but calm. There was not one word of protest about Mindy—you smiled and said, "It's all right, Mother. We are trusting the Lord." That was all. You then turned on some beautiful symphony music, lay down on the divan, closed your eyes and did not speak for over an hour. Barbara was just as magnificent. How I thank God that He sent you that girl, Tom! If you had looked the whole world over, you couldn't have chosen a finer mate. What a blessing to know that my child is married to a fine Christian.

How could I ever forget the look on your faces when the orthopedic doctor in San Francisco said "She will walk. . . . I'll guarantee it!" He even let us take Mindy home. She didn't have to spend a single night alone in a strange hospital. "He careth for His own." Amen!

The tears of relief, joy, and gratefulness on your shining faces was almost too much to bear—I felt as if I were going to burst.

Then there was the eventful night before our opening at Madison Square Garden Rodeo. We had encountered opposition to our Christian spot on our song program and had to take a stand on it. Just before starting back to our hotel, one of the cowboys came into our dressing room, and in tears asked us to pray for his little boy who was dying of leukemia, out West. Through the kindness of friends, he was able to fly out to see the little lad, but the doctors had pronounced the case hopeless and this poor cowboy was in a bad way. We had prayer with him and started wearily for the hotel. As we walked into our room, my eye fell on a telephone message that read, "Call Tom—Important—Little Candy very sick."

My heart sank. Little Candy was your second baby girl, and reminded me so much of Robin. When I got you on the phone in Yreka, you tried to be matter-of-fact about it, but your voice nearly broke when you said little Candy was a severe diabetic, had a bad virus infection, and was in serious condition in the hospital in Medford, fifty miles from your home. You said for me not to worry, that God had the situation in hand, and you would call me Sunday, after they had treated her for four days.

This time I didn't break down nor utter any protest, but I knew God wanted me to act quickly to get Candy into the hands of a diabetes specialist. The Lord guided me all the following day on telephoning the necessary people to have your little family flown to Los Angeles, and to have Candy taken to Children's Hospital for immediate treatment. We were to open at the Garden at 8:30 P.M., and at 6:00 P.M. I heard your relieved voice from Los Angeles saying, "Everything is fine—Candy is responding, and we praise the Lord." Again, "He careth for His own."

I should say He *did* care for you! The doctors said you should live in Los Angeles, where you would be near doctor and hospitals specializing in the handling of diabetes—and there you were, at the opening of a school term, with all the teaching jobs filled in Los Angeles. It meant you had to give up your job in Yreka, sell your little house, and come down to Los Angeles with no job. Well, you left Barbara and the children with her mother, and went back to settle your affairs in Yreka. And what happened? A man drove up to your house the day you were leaving to come down here, and paid you in *cash* the amount of money you had put into that house! Another man came and bought your old "jalopy" Model T Ford for $100, both transactions occurring the day you *left* for Los Angeles!

There was not one teaching job open in the Los Angeles school system, but a music teacher in the Glendale area decided suddenly, "for some unexplained reason," that he wanted to retire. There were several aspirants, but you qualified, Tom—"He careth for His own."

Little Mindy walks beautifully, runs, skips, and is a delightful five-year-old. Candy, now almost three, has made her adjustment to diabetes beautifully, and although keeping her insulin and food balance is tricky, you and Barbara have taken it in your stride and never fail to praise God for His goodness to you. You have prayed for her healing only if it be in accordance with the divine purpose of our Lord. Yes, Tom, you are glorifying God through infirmity and you count it a joy and privilege!

Then there is radiant little Nancy Hamilton and her inspiring mother, who have traveled the way of the cross for fourteen years, through extreme infirmity. Nancy was born with a rare blood disease, with deformed legs and hands. After twelve years of suffering through some forty operations, her legs were amputated last year, and now her hands and torso have telltale signs. Nancy and her brave Christian mother live above their circumstances, in Christ, and they have blessed countless lives. Nancy is like a ray of sunshine, and her angelic and serene face belies her condition. "He careth for His own!" They have complete trust in the Lord, and He has met every need. Theirs is an incredible story of Christian faith. Whenever I am "dragging a little," Nancy and her Mom just seem to "drop by," and what a boost they give my spirits! Nancy never has complained of her malady, but counts it a privilege to be a weak vessel through which our blessed Lord may reach hungry souls.

Why do Christians suffer? *To glorify God!*

Lovingly yours,
Mother.

Dear Tom

I get so many letters from dear folks wanting to adopt a child, and saying that they have been on waiting lists for months with adoption agencies and are unable to understand why they cannot get a child. You know, there are children who can be adopted faster, but sometimes they are deemed unadoptable by reason of nationality or some kind of handicap. I am sure that Roy and I would not have obtained little Dodie and Sandy so quickly had Dodie not been mostly Indian, and Sandy physically handicapped at the time.

It was hard for many fine folks to understand why we wanted to adopt an Indian child. Well, Roy is part Choctaw himself, for one reason—but mainly it was because we wanted one who might have a harder time being adopted, since she was in a minority class. The same was true of Sandy, with his physical handicap caused by early, severe rickets. We do not take any credit for adopting these children: the credit goes to the

Lord, who burdened our hearts with their plight. He deserves the credit. Had we not been trying to serve Him, we might have tried to adopt different children—but how grateful I am that we didn't! Those two children have done far more for us than we have done, or ever can do for them. Dodie, our little papoose, now almost four, and Sandy, now eight, are really our children under God. We believe that God is the real father of all our children and we are just caretakers for Him.

Another child, a fifteen-year-old Scottish girl named Marion, is also sharing our home as a foster child. I am "Mama" to Marion, and Roy is "Daddy." She has been here for only a year and a half, but she is definitely a part of our family, just like the other children, and it is hard to imagine being without any of them.

Not long ago, Reverend Dick Halverson, addressing our Hollywood Christian Group, said he would never be the same after visiting Korea and seeing the plight of Korean orphans. He and Bob Pierce brought their film to our home and we were privileged to adopt (by long distance, through World Vision, Inc.) some of these little children—by sending ten dollars per month per child for its upkeep. I wish you could read their letters to us. We are their mama and daddy, by mail. The church orphanages are doing a magnificent work with these children; they are teaching them the love of Jesus and caring for them physically and spiritually—on very limited means. Our adopted Korean children, (some of them blinded by the war), in their Christmas letters to us almost without exception said, "You must be having a wonderful Christmas—and enjoying your healthy body." This struck at my heart, as letter after letter spoke almost with awe of "a healthy body." We, who take a healthy body for granted and complain because we can't have everything work à la push-button in our homes and cars! These children all said they wanted to grow up to be good Christians, to make a better world. Only ten dollars a month to foster a child like that! Why, that's not even pin money to most people!

Many of these children saw their parents killed before their very eyes. Only the love of Christ can dim that painful memory. There are full-blooded Korean kiddies, as well as those of mixed blood, in the orphanages. Many are adoptable into American homes. With so many child-hungry but barren couples in America, waiting so long on adoption agencies here, why can't we open our homes and hearts to these children and give them a Christian country and home? The orphanages are full in Korea, and yet there are hundreds of homeless tots, many dying from neglect and starvation. If we could just bring the adoptable ones over here and place them in welcome homes, there would be room in the orphanages in Korea to save the ones who are "on the outside looking in." There are beautiful half-American, half-Korean children. I have seen pictures of many of them and they are lovely. We have applied for a little girl Dodie's age, to raise with Dodie, if it be the Lord's will. You know, I believe the spirit of our American boys who fathered many of these children, some spilling their blood on Korean soil, would rejoice to see their country take their war children and teach them Christian peace. "Suffer the little children to come unto me, for of such is the kingdom of heaven."

Our Lord told us to care for the afflicted and the fatherless. That is a divine commission, and I am sure that the wonderful Christian man in Oregon, Mr. Holt, who adopted eight of these little children, must be *very* happy.

Not long ago I was asked to speak on Christianity in the home at the Youth for Christ annual family night. My, that was a large order, and I certainly was not qualified to preach! There was a lot on my heart about this matter, though—and it was a privilege to share some of my thoughts with the fine families represented there. Much of my thinking was based on Psalm 127: "Except the Lord build the house, they labour in vain that build it: except the Lord keep the city, the watchman waketh but in vain." Or Ephesians 5: "Be ye therefore followers of God, as dear children; And walk in love, as Christ also hath loved us, and hath given himself for us an offering and a sacrifice to God for a sweetsmelling savour. . . . Wherefore be ye not unwise, but understanding what the will of the Lord is. . . . Speaking to yourselves in psalms and hymns and spiritual songs, singing and making melody in your heart to the Lord; Giving thanks always for all things unto God and the Father in the name of our Lord Jesus Christ; Submitting yourselves one to another in the fear of God. Wives, submit yourselves unto your own husbands, as unto the Lord. . . . Husbands, love your wives, even as Christ also loved the church, and gave himself for it. . . . Children, obey your parents in the Lord: for this is right. Honour thy father and mother; which is the first commandment with promise; That it may be well with thee, and thou mayest live long on the earth. And, ye fathers, provoke not your children to wrath: but bring them up in the nurture and admonition of the Lord."

This Scripture is very clear as to what the attitude of the family should be one to another. "Except the Lord build the house, they labour in vain that build it." How true I have found that to be! I can honestly and humbly say to you that if Jesus Christ had not come into our lives eight years ago, our marriage probably would not have survived. Shortly after giving my heart and life to Christ, someone sent me a little book titled, *In His Steps.* That book impressed and greatly benefited me spiritually. It was the story of a few consecrated Christians who made a pact to conduct their lives in every situation on the basis of "What would Jesus do?" It is a wonderful book and I wish every Christian would read it. Just think what one family could accomplish for the Lord, if each member would really try to do what he thought Jesus would have him to do! No telling how far their good influence would reach. I wish you would read *In His Steps.*

It has been said, "To err is human; to forgive, divine." Forgiveness *is* divine, because our Lord Jesus Christ commanded it. Among lots of our young people, rebellion against all authority seems to be the order of the day. I was talking to Dr. Bob Pierce, of World Vision, last week, and the subject of juvenile delinquency came up. He had seen the picture "Rebel Without a Cause." He said that actually, in the story, the parents were the real delinquents and the children simply rebels. If this was the case in the story, in my humble opinion the little rebels *did* have a cause—their parents! The Bible says "Children, obey your parents in the Lord." I have told our children the reason they should obey us is because God said so, in His Word, the Holy Bible. By the same token, we parents should not deliberately anger our children. The term, "provoke to wrath," I believe, means the conscious repetition of irritating acts or nagging until a child explodes with anger. Sometimes we parents forget that our children are growing up, and that we are actually just their caretakers for God until they are old enough to think for themselves, after reaching the age of accountability.

Not long ago, Cheryl and Marion were arguing about "going steady" with a boy. I listened for a while and then impatiently complained, "Why should you worry about going steady with any boy, at fifteen? You have plenty of time to worry about settling down with one boy!" Marion pursed her lips and asked, "Mama, when you were young, didn't you ever do *anything?*" Did that set me back on my heels! With horror, I discovered she thought I was *old!* Right then and there I decided that I had better start *remembering* some things I did!

You know, Christianity is wonderful in the home, Tom. No matter what difficulty you have had during the daytime with any member of the family, when you join hands during evening prayer time, and ask God to forgive you and help you, everything has a way of smoothing out! The Bible says "Let not the sun go down on your wrath." Sometimes we get in just under the wire! The important thing is that we have a place to go where we can settle our differences, and our place is one of justice and mercy—and we all become one in Him! 'Tis a blessed thing to be a part of a family. God was very loving when He instituted the human family for us to enjoy.

It is still more blessed when the members of the family love, respect and *trust* each other. The wonderful thing about a Christian family is that they are all pressing onward together toward the highest possible goal—everlasting life in the Lord Jesus Christ. When Jesus comes into the heart and He is put first in a family, then petty differences are just naturally ironed out as that family finds communion in Him. If one is a Christian and the others are not, I believe with all my heart that the Christian should never stop witnessing and living for Christ before his loved ones. The Christian plants the seed and God gives the increase. Sometimes we have to plant a whole garden! Even then it seems we sit and wait a long time. Then suddenly there's not a shower, but a rainstorm (lots of trouble, maybe big trouble for the loved one we're praying for)—and we fear that maybe our seeds are all washed away. Then, just as we are about to give up, we see a tiny green shoot of life coming up. If we are wise, we will tend it patiently and carefully, so that it might reach full bloom and bear fruit.

This is faith—the Christian faith—and it works! I've seen it, time and time again. What a blessed heritage we Americans have! Our country was founded by men of deep Christian faith, who believed in liberty and justice for all, in equality, in the righteousness of Jesus Christ. Tom, I believe the United States of America is as great and will always be just as great as her faith in Jesus Christ. Our wonderful country is made up of Christian individuals in Christian families, and faith must be in the heart of each individual—faith in what our country stands for!

The providence of God is amazing, Tom. He provides for His children and He protects them against terrific odds sometimes. Just recently this was brought home to me in a very tangible way. I learned a great lesson ten days before this past Christmas, and was astounded at God's protection. Someone had sent us a pretty Christmas candle centerpiece, resplendent with frosted red ribbons, bright ornaments, and an attractive branch of snow-covered wood. I lighted it and placed it atop our television set as a festive and cheery Christmas note. As a rule I am the last to bed, and I handle the turn-out-the-light chores. Dad Rogers was up in Marysville, duck hunting—and being rather weary from a very full day, I excused myself at 7:30 P.M., after having prayers at our altar, asking Marion to "douse the lights."

As my good friend and secretary, Pat O'Shea, was taking a couple of days' rest from driving the girls into Canoga Park to school, I intended rising at 6:45 A.M. to do that chore. At four in the morning, the insistent voice of Cheryl, our eldest, boomed through our bedroom intercom set: "Mama, get up, quick!" I stumbled over to the speaker and grumbled, "I have three more hours of sleep; what's the matter?" She said, with studied calmness, "Mama, the house is on fire." In a fog, I grabbed a housecoat and slippers and made my way toward the living room. Stepping into the hallway, I got my first bad lungful of smoke. The living room was suffused by an evil, red glow—and suddenly I remembered my precious little Dodie and Marion in the room adjoining. Coughing,

I threw open their door, praying they wouldn't be harmed—to find them coughing and groping for robes and slippers. Grabbing the first clothes I could find, I threw them on the girls and told them to run through the living room, not looking back, and to keep going to the pasture at the back of the house. Cheryl, Linda, Dusty and Sandy were already outside. Linda had called the Canoga Park Fire Department. The television had burned completely down through the floor; the piano and all surrounding carpeting were afire and one of the huge ceiling beams had just started to blaze. I suddenly remembered that the intense heat of the fire was perilously close to the wires leading to our huge central heating unit which was in the basement practically under the fire. Any minute I expected an explosion. Betty Ordono, our housekeeper, said in a shaking voice, "It must have been the hand of the Lord shaking me, for I seemed to hear a voice say, 'Get up! Get up!' " She said when she stepped into the kitchen and dining area, which adjoins the living room, the smoke was so thick she couldn't even see the white refrigerator across the room. She then summoned Cheryl and Linda to call me, as I was on the opposite end of our long, rambling ranch house.

Cheryl hopped into the jeep and drove down to the entrance to our ranch, to point the way up to the house should the fire department have trouble finding us. Sure enough, they had been knocking on doors along Lassen Avenue—our place is a little out of the way. How good that big, red engine looked, pulling up the hill to our house! They had the fire put out in just a few minutes, and said it was a miracle the whole house had not caught fire. The insurance company said the same thing. They were incredulous, when they saw the effects of the intense heat, that the fire stayed localized, particularly since there were two old-fashioned kerosene lamps, full to the brim with kerosene, sitting on top of the piano. They never exploded!

Tom, the hand of the Lord stayed the fire. Just a week previous, I had been watching a picture on television about an alcoholic mother who carelessly dropped a cigarette on the rug, endangering the life of her small daughter upstairs. I shuddered when I saw it, thinking to myself, "This would never happen to me! I would never do a thing like *that!* How could a mother care so little for her child as to become an alcoholic?" There I was, sitting judgment upon people who had a weakness for liquor, instead of realizing that but for the grace of God, I could perhaps be that very same person. Do you see what I mean about learning a lesson in humility? Just one week later, from fatigue, I was careless of my own responsibility for lighting a candle—leaving it to a teenager to put out. Well, it taught me several lessons—and I was one humble and thankful mother the next day, when I considered what *might* have happened!

Lovingly yours,
Mother.

Dear Tom

Tom, we should be so grateful to God that we are a Christian country, despite contrary propaganda! Even if we, as a Christian country, are prone to fall short of the Christian ideal at times, we nevertheless have the greatest system of government on the face of the earth. Why? Because it is based on the *sovereignty* of God and the brotherhood of man. If every one of us based all our decisions and actions on what we truly believe is the Christian way, we would uphold our Constitution in such a strong manner that the entire world would see that Jesus Christ is, indeed, the Way, the Truth, and the Life. We, as Christians, *must practice* the brotherhood of man. We must first of all stop the fighting among the divisions of Christendom. *Surely* we can agree as brothers under Christ, our Lord. We all live, humanly, in different houses, but under the same sky.

So many people of different Christian denominations send me the arguments in favor of their denomination.

Tom, no one branch of the universal church of Christ has all the truth in its keeping, *for the truth is all revealed for all of us in the Holy Bible!*

Billy Graham has just been severely scored for putting his emphasis "on the Bible before the church." Well, all I can say is, "Praise the Lord!" The *Word* of God *was* before the church—the first recorded Word of God was given to Moses. The *Word* was *first*—and Jesus Christ was the *Word* who came *before* the organized Christian church at Antioch. Here we are, haggling about which should have pre-eminence, while Satan laughs and entices the bewildered onlooker into his realm of the dead, where he is taught to glorify the flesh, to eat, drink and be merry, for tomorrow he may die, and after that—nothing! Every time the flesh, instead of the Creator, is set upon a pedestal, havoc follows—for as St. Paul said, "In the flesh dwelleth no good thing." Only God is perfect, unchanging. We are constantly changing, but if we have placed our faith and trust in the Lord Jesus Christ, ". . . we all, with open face beholding as in a glass the glory of the Lord, are changed into the same image from glory to glory, even as by the Spirit of the Lord" (II Corinthians 3:18).

Lovingly yours,
Mother.

Dear Tom

We went to Commerce, Texas, this past week to present the Roy Rogers Safety Award for the best safety program in an elementary school in 1955. Wheeler Elementary School certainly showed what perseverance and faith in something right can accomplish. The children put on a fine program for us, and as the little ones sang, "The Bible Tells Me So," I got quite a lump in my throat. As I looked into their bright, happy and trusting faces, many things crowded my mind.

For instance, of all the people on the face of the earth, we Americans should be the happiest and most grateful. We have a precious heritage—a free, Christian country, a country believing in the Fatherhood of God and the brotherhood of man. We learned this precept from our Elder Brother and Saviour, Jesus Christ, who told us to love our neighbors as ourselves. This means that we really are our brother's keeper—and the keeper of his safety. The laws of our land are decreed to protect the rights of every individual. Learning to "play it safe" early in life, by obeying our parents and safety rules, helps boys and girls all through their lives in making small and big decisions. By considering our own safety and the safety of others, I believe, we live a happier, longer and more successful life.

This present-day business of boys and girls thinking they are "chicken" if they aren't selfishly reckless is a disgrace to the American way of life. We in America do not believe that life is cheap, as do so many other peoples. We believe every living soul is precious in the sight of our Maker. Where have we failed our children, that they think it is a noble thing to endanger the lives of innocent people by playing their imbecile game of "chicken"? Where did they get this strange and twisted idea? The policeman who drove us down from Dallas told us of a suicidal teen-age game played here occasionally, called "Octopus." It seems that one person operates the brakes, one the steering wheel, and one the emergency brake, one the horn, and one the lights. One "operator" never knows what the others will do. However, in case of emergency, he who grabs his part of the mechanism first is "chicken"! This ridiculous operation is a pitiable reflection of the appalling and apparent disunity in the home, the churches, and other organizations.

Our nation is a Christian nation; the laws of our land are based on the Bible. There was a day in this country when all schools had chapel, where the Bible was read and prayer was offered to our God. Even if a child came from a home in which the Bible was never opened, or where there was no church attendance or no professed religion, at least in school the child had the opportunity of hearing the Holy Scriptures on which the laws of the land are based. "Train up a child in the way he shall go, and when he is old, he will not depart from it." Why expect the Juvenile Courts of our land to perform miracles in the personalities of wayward boys or girls, when the early impressionable years are devoid of spiritual training? Why is it unconstitutional to read the Bible in our public schools when a person on the witness stand in our courts takes his oath on the Bible? If the Bible is recognized by our courts of law which are expected to correct lawlessness, surely our schools could recognize the authority of the Bible in the government of our children! If our President can pray, surely the children of this land can bow their heads to the God of our forefathers!

Not long ago I received a letter from a confused teenager who said she couldn't seem to "get through to God" in her prayers. So many young people write about that! The wonderful thing about prayer, however, is that we do not have to depend on our "feeling," but on the promise that Jesus made when He said to ask the Father in His name and the prayer would be answered. Now God is not a mail-order house, but He is our Father! We shouldn't order something from Him expecting Him to send just the right size, color, and price, on a specified date. He will answer the order in His own good time, which is different from ours—and the answer may not be the answer we expect. But it will be the right answer for us because the Bible asks what Father, when his son asks for a fish would give him a serpent? No, our Father gives us only what is good, because He loves us. Sometimes the gift wrapping looks a bit strange to us, but the gift itself is always perfect. When we are in Eternity, we will probably be quite abashed when we see, with Him, the "end from the beginning"—and we will readily understand and praise His wisdom in handling our earthly affairs. Jesus said, "He that hath eyes to see, let him see." God is speaking to us constantly, if our spiritual eyes and ears are open to the wonders He performs constantly. Many things we look upon as "coincidence" are really God's superb timing!

Lovingly yours,
Mother.

Dear Tom

Oh, Tom, today Roy and I went to the Children's Hospital, and I saw things that brought tears to my eyes and heart. There was a precious little girl with big, soft, brown eyes in a white, pinched little face, and a pitifully emaciated body—a congenital heart condition. She was five years old, and I picked her up as if she were a baby of one year. Her mother said she is one of nine children and that she is the "hub" of the family. Her life expectancy was six months at time of birth, and her heart is inoperable. Her mother said, "Oh, she is an angel visiting us—we all know it, and are thankful for her being here this long." That mother had complete peace and understanding. What a job that little angelic ambassador has done in that family! Praise the Lord!

There was another more pathetic mother, standing at the glass window, crying her heart out over her small boy, who is a "free bleeder." There was another infant going to surgery for a heart operation, and a little twelve-year-old girl, unconscious from a compound skull fracture caused when a runaway horse knocked her to the pavement. Tom, there is no surer way to a mother's heart than through her child. Although I saw anxiety in the faces of the parents, there was also acceptance and peace and love. I heard once that tears are God's rainfall to soften the human heart—that's the time He can really plant a garden of faith; and if the mind will water that garden with hope instead of doubt, the beauty of that heart will bless abundantly. One of the cruelest blows a parent can deliver to himself is to think that his child suffered in vain. If that child's suffering has caused the parent to turn sincerely to God, then the child's suffering was *glorious*. A little child is in the kingdom at the moment of his birth because Jesus said, "Of such is the kingdom of heaven." We leave the kingdom when we cease to be children, and by choice embrace the knowledge of evil. We become children again when we decide that our worldly knowledge counts for nothing and that the only Truth is God and His Christ; then the cross of Christ takes us across the bridge to the kingdom again.

Lovingly yours,
Mother.

Dear Tom

It's Good Friday, and here we are flying to Washington, D.C., to participate in a special sunrise service Easter morning, commemorating the resurrection of our blessed Lord Jesus Christ. Roy and I, Art Rush, and the Sons of the Pioneers are all together on the plane, rehearsing our hymn with the big choir. Our good friend, Billy Graham, will preach—how wonderful to hear him again! He's just returned from the Orient, and what a thrill it will be to hear of his great Christian experience there. We understand he and Bev Shea spent some time with our prospective Korean-American daughter in Seoul, where she is waiting for someone to bring her over to us. They sent us her pictures, and she is a darling! She is just a few months younger than Dodie, and Dodie is "champing at the bit" with impatience for her "sister" to get here.

Tom, we have prayed much about this addition to our family—and we believe it is according to the will of God.

As in the case of Dodie, we have already named our little Korean blossom "Deborah," before she even gets here. Her bed is ready, right next to Dodie's, and the children have for some time now spoken of "Debbie" as if she is already installed in our family. She is truly a war orphan; her mother died from the ravages of disease and her father was lost in the war. We pray that we will not fail our Lord in raising her for His purpose.

I have no qualms about the loving acceptance of little Debbie into our hearts and home; it will happen easily and naturally, as was the case with Dodie. Our family believes in the brotherhood of man under the Fatherhood of God, in Christ, who died for *all* men, regardless of race, creed, or color. I do not believe Jesus "looks down" on any man—else why the story of the Good Samaritan? America has long been a blessed haven to hunted, oppressed, and weary souls, and I pray that many of these little bewildered orphans of war will somehow find their way to the "Promised Land" they so desperately need.

Yes, I know it seems that we have "enough children" already—but there is still room in the hearts and, I might add, room in the house! All my life I have thought with pleasure of the wonderful times I had as a child when we visited my grandparents, on both sides of the family. There were seven children in Dad's family and eight in Mom's. They got along, by the grace of God, and so will we! This will make seven children at the Double R Bar—with you already "married off," and one waiting in the heavenlies.

As the plane roars along above the clouds, I am thinking that I have an apology to make, via telephone, tonight, to Dusty and Sandy. You know, all the children earn their allowances because we believe in their accepting some responsibility in keeping up the home, and at the same time, we want to give them an incentive to work by paying them for their chores. They do not get paid for making their own beds and picking up their own clothes and toys—only when they do "extra-curricular" jobs. Dusty is supposed to set the table at night, and Sandy dries the dishes; for this they each get a small amount per day. They give ten per cent of it to Sunday school, and I must admit they do it gracefully! The girls take turns clearing the table and serving, vacuuming and dusting, and putting Dodie to bed on days when we are short of help and I am busy with outside work. The girls get paid so much per job, too, but none of the children gets paid unless he or she does the job. This money they may spend as they choose. Well, Dusty got rather frustrated because he had so many extra places to set this week, and "conveniently" didn't hear the summons to set the table. Therefore, I docked him four days' allowance. The same thing happened with Sandy's dish drying. However, I now realize that dinner was not right on schedule during the past week (Easter vacation) and that the boys got a little "mixed up." Therefore, I will have to apologize and make up the deficit on my return Monday. You know, Tom, I pray the Lord will always convict me of a definite sense of wrong when I have misjudged my children and give me the grace to say, "I'm sorry, kids"—because it is a slap to a child's sense of security when a parent fails to "make it right" when the parent is wrong. I have to say, "Forgive me," pretty often, but what a relief when that little face relaxes and softens back into childish, trusting serenity. A child needs to learn the blessing of saying, "I'm sorry," because repentance and forgiveness are commands from our Lord Jesus Christ. Forgiveness and love go hand in hand.

The forthrightness of children is refreshing! Dodie and I were flying in to New York to see Roy last fall at Madison Square Garden (the other children were in school); the weather was pretty choppy, and there was lightning in the southern sky. Dodie had never seen lightning before, and her large, black olive eyes snapped with fearful curiosity! "Mama, what dat?" she asked; to which I replied, "Why, that's God's way of speaking to us, Dodie—He's flashing His light at the world to tell us that it might rain!" She pondered this for a moment, eyes glued on the dark sky. The lightning flashed again. Suddenly Dodie called uncertainly, "God?" She waited, and then louder, "God?" Another wait—then, "God! Answer me!" By this time, nearby fellow passengers were struggling to hold back their laughter. Then she said, "Mama, sing 'Jesus Loves Me' loud, so He can hear!" The drone of the plane was loud, so I could oblige my child without disturbing other passengers, and she was satisfied.

Actually, we never quite outgrow the desire for audibly hearing God's voice, or for a physical presence that we can touch with our hands. It's like the child who said, "I want a God with a face!" That's the humanity in us, even when we know better! "By *faith* are ye justified. . . ." —by faith in the unseen, to do that which is best for us.

Lovingly yours,
Mother.

Dear Tam

Being a parent is a wonderful but awesome responsibility. It has been said that "Mother love sometimes becomes 'smother love!' " I pray constantly that I will merely water the plant and have the sense to stand back and watch God give the increase. We have no right to *live* our children's lives. God must live in them and operate through them. This is very difficult for the aggressive type of parent, who wants the child to succeed in gratifying his own wishes instead of God's. This is a hard statement and I am saying it to myself first, because I, too, am guilty at times of daydreaming about the future of these children. They must be encouraged, but not pushed. Many children and adults go through life feeling they are failures because they have not measured up to the expectations of their parents or friends, when perhaps they are succeeding right along in accomplishing the holy purpose of God, because His ways are not our ways—and what sometimes seems a failure to us is success to God.

It is now Monday noon, and we are returning to Los Angeles aboard the "Statesman" airliner. What a thrilling Easter week end! Tom, I wish every child in our nation could have the privilege of really seeing our capital the way Roy and I have just seen it. We are deeply grateful for it and we have come away with a deeper consecration to our Lord and our country because of it.

First of all, we had the pleasure of meeting Senator and Mrs. Price Daniel of Texas, and lunching with them at the Senate Restaurant—and *we* got some autographs from the Senators! What fine-looking statesmen they were! In my heart, I breathed a prayer for each of these men who courageously chart the course of our nation. We had the famous Navy bean soup, and I might add, it is excellent bean soup, made with ham hocks and onions, and has been listed on the back of the restaurant menu for many years—a Senate lunchroom tradition.

Lots of folks deplore tradition, but where would history be without it? What is tradition anyway? It is a belief and practice we believe to be good and which we faithfully pass along to our children. Some traditions are added to, as time goes on, and some traditions are dropped in the sincere conviction that they are wrong for that particular day. But tradition is still a part of our culture. Those who would throw all our "outworn traditions" away should be careful they don't throw away our great American heritage of religious freedom! That would be like throwing out the baby with the bath water.

Senator Daniel is the head of "International Christian Leadership," and we were so pleased to learn of his fine Christian work in prayer groups within the government. He told us of their weekly prayer breakfasts, where they each read the Bible, discuss it, and pray over their responsibilities in representing the people of the United States. This is the real strength of our country, Tom—"God is our strength and our refuge"—and these men work on this holy promise. I know that Reverend Richard Halverson, our Hollywood Christian Group Chaplain, is going to enjoy thoroughly his new call to I.C.L., working with Senator Price Daniel. It seems highly probable that Texas will call Senator Daniel home to govern the state, and if that happens, I believe Washington will feel keenly the loss of this dedicated man. He and his charming lady told us about a wonderful family practice: each day they and their children read a portion of the Bible and have prayer—and on Sunday, they have a real Christian "pow-wow." They read and discuss a certain portion of Scripture; then each confesses something he has done wrong during the week, and also something good that has happened. Then they all pray. I'll wager there are no nervous breakdowns in *this* family! This is an excellent practice and makes for the finest family relationships. We do this in our home (the confessional part) occasionally, but I think we will establish a steady rule for it each day before dinner, when we have our round-table Grace. So many things come up to bother one during the week, and sometimes we carry little unresolved feelings of wrong or guilt for too long, and they keep festering like boils in the subconscious until they explode in an apparently unreasonable fit of temper. How much better to haul them out at the end of the day, either say "I'm sorry" or "I forgive you," and ask the

Lord to heal the abrasion by His Holy Spirit. "The family who prays together *stays* together." How true!

Next on our agenda was one of the big thrills of our lives—we visited the White House, met our beloved President Eisenhower and his charming First Lady. Tom, how I praise God for President Eisenhower. He is kindness personified. When he smiles, and that is most of the time, it's like watching the sunrise! He is such a humble man and obviously consecrated to the service of God and his country. It was the birthday of little David, the President's grandson. Roy and I sang some Western songs to the little cowboy-hatted celebrants, and then Roy presented David with a three and one-half foot boat, a replica of his grandfather's Yellow Jacket fishing boat. David, so his charming mother told us, is a water enthusiast, and he was thrilled with Roy's present. The President and Mrs. Eisenhower are devoted grandparents, and our hearts were warmed to know that this fine example of Christian American family occupies the White House today. I was particularly impressed to see that David received but a modest amount of birthday presents, actually less than most people would imagine, inasmuch as he is the grandson of the President of the United States. This was a very significant thing to me—this family does not worship the material things of life. God bless them and strengthen them. Our country needs folks like this.

The President and Mrs. Eisenhower personally showed us through their living quarters. We saw the Lincoln Room, the famous huge four-poster bed, and there over the fireplace stood the written testimony of the great and strong-hearted President who believed in the equality of every man under God in this country; the plaque states that, in this room, President Lincoln signed the Emancipation Proclamation. As I looked into the face of today's dedicated President Eisenhower, there was the same firmness of conviction about liberty and justice for all. It is often said today that the United States presidency is a killing job. This blessed man has suffered a heart attack, but our God saw fit to raise him up again, and with all my heart I believe that President Eisenhower is and will be supported by the Everlasting Arms to carry out God's purpose in our nation. "Not by power or by might, but by *my spirit,* saith the Lord." This was the message stamped on my heart as we left the White House.

Saturday night we were on television with Reverend Joe Uhrig's "Hand to Heaven" program. Reverend Uhrig was responsible for bringing us to Washington for the Easter services, and we are deeply grateful to him for one of the finest and most inspiring days we have ever known. The Sons of the Pioneers and Les Barnett, at the organ, were with us. Reverend Uhrig told us that "Rock of Ages" is the President's favorite hymn, so we sang and dedicated it to the Eisenhowers.

I met another "little angel" at the telecast, Tom. Her name is Pamela Springman, and her father is the soloist and musical director of "Hand to Heaven" telecast. Little Pam has a rare blood disease, seemingly akin to leukemia. She was born with it; she is now five and a half, and must have a blood transfusion every two weeks. They call her the "Red Cross Girl." It seems that her blood cannot replenish itself; hence the transfusions. This child is a mighty influence on the lives of her parents, who are surrendered Christians. Little Pam has a lovely voice and uses it to the glory of the Lord. She is a beautiful child, with wide-apart, brown eyes, and long brown curls. Her smile is breath-taking, and everyone around her basks in the warmth of her caressing spirit. Little Pam seems constantly to express the inspiring words of the 104th Psalm: "I will sing unto the Lord as long as I live: I will sing praise to my God while I have my being. My meditation of him shall be sweet: I will be glad in the Lord." Pam *is* glad in the Lord, despite the transfusions. Your little Candy, in spite of the jab of an insulin-filled needle twice a day, still joyfully sings, "A sunbeam, a sunbeam, Jesus wants me for a sunbeam—a sunbeam, a sunbeam, I'll be a sunbeam for Him," and Candy *is* a sunbeam in all our lives. She is a joy despite her diabetic affliction. God compensates. Praise His name!

We have just flown through a rather impertinent thunderstorm. I had to stop writing and hold on for a few minutes. The co-pilot announced that we were flying by radar (visibility nothing!), but we were not to worry for we would stay on our course and be out of the storm in an hour. Now I am looking out of my window at brilliant sunshine and fleecy clouds again. It's like the Christian life, Tom—Christ is our radar, and He keeps us on our course. Though the weather is rough at times and we feel "closed in," He brings us safely through to the sunshine. It's only when we doubt our radar, and venture off the course, that we are likely to have a smashup.

The Easter sunrise service at Walter Reed Hospital was glorious—the morning sky was ablaze with light, the air crisp. My brother and his wife, from New York, were with us, and I was wishing Mom could have been there too. We met Dr. Billy Graham at the home of General Heaton, had coffee, and then marched onto the field for the services. The presentation of the Colors was beautiful! Fague Springman, father of little Pam, sang "The Lord's Prayer." Then Roy and I gave a brief Easter testimony and sang our arrangements of "The Old Rugged Cross," "Christ Arose," and "He Lives!" Billy Graham, possessed by the Holy Spirit, proclaimed the Christian triumph of the empty tomb—what a message! People were spellbound—the only sound, save his voice, was the glad, joyous song of birds over the platform. Truly, Tom, Billy Graham is our Noah, our John the Baptist, our Paul. God has really anointed this man. The world feels it, wherever he goes.

After the service we all had breakfast in the cafeteria, and Billy spoke to us again—what an Easter feast! Following breakfast, Roy and I visited the spinal injuries ward. We were appalled to learn that most of these hopelessly injured boys were the victims of automobile smashups. Our servicemen forever crippled by automobiles! This auto carelessness must be corrected—and we, as parents, must first set the example and then follow up during the teen-age driving instruction period. Somehow, we must get across the fact that it is not smart to be reckless. It is smart to be square with our fellow man, by observing traffic regulations and speed limits. Those paralyzed boys were a pitiful sight. We saw two teen-age boys, also, with brain tumors. They looked so healthy—but in a matter of months the malady will take over. I want to write those boys about the Lord Jesus Christ, and send them our testimony tract.

Chaplain Bradley then took us to the Chapel and we gave a testimony there, and sang. I told those convalescent boys about my former visit to Walter Reed Hospital, when you were stationed there in 1946; and I told them that although I wasn't a Christian then, you were, and that you were the one who brought me to Christ in 1948—and that your faith in the Lord had helped you "stay on your course" in the Army. We arrived at the National Presbyterian Church at 10:45 and heard Dr. Elson preach on "Truth Vindicated." He said they tried to kill Truth by nailing it to a tree, and putting it in a tomb, but it arose and has lived through the centuries to convict human beings of sin. It was a powerful message. President and Mrs. Eisenhower were there, and we had the pleasure of greeting them, along with Dr. Elson, after the service.

Sunday night we gave our testimony at Constitution Hall at two services. The people were attentive and responsive. Fague Springman sang, "I Walked Today Where Jesus Walked," and it was magnificent in poignancy, particularly because Fague *is* walking the path of Gethsemane all the time, surrendering his will for little Pam to the will of the Lord. Pam's mother is a fine pianist and accompanies her husband and child. Someone was worried about the disturbance of some babies crying during the testimonies. Why, babies are in the kingdom, and they couldn't really hamper the Holy Spirit anyway! Those parents probably could not be there unless they brought the babies. There were quite a few decisions made to follow Christ, and we were grateful for the working of the Holy Spirit and that God saw fit to let us serve Him, in Constitution Hall in Washington, D.C., on Easter Day. We shall treasure it always.

I praise and thank the Lord Jesus Christ for His gift of Everlasting Life, through the Cross of Calvary and His resurrection. I *know* my Redeemer lives, because I see Him living in the heart and life of America. In following Him, I too have experienced my Garden of Gethsemane and my Calvary—but it was glorious, because He was with me. He brought me safely through to the resurrection of a new life, filled with love, service, hope, and Christian peace, the peace that passes all understanding. Yes, I *know* in whom I have believed!

Lovingly yours,
Mother.

Dear Tom

Well, here I am, flat on my back with old-fashioned "flu"! Had to cancel out my part on the NBC color television show on baseball tomorrow—"Paw" and the Pioneers will appear. It will be fun to watch Roy in his bright red Indian shirt, as he "kibitzes" with the Little Leaguers and Trigger! Isn't it wonderful that civic organizations are backing such a wholesome American sport for our youth? Little League takes the boys through the adolescent period, and gives them a healthy interest and goal outside their school hours. The boys are taught how to have fun in fair play and square-shooting, and to respect and abide by the rules—factors so essential to good citizenship.

You know, Tom, most of the artists' conceptions of our Lord Jesus Christ tend to give him a look of sorrow and compassion. The Bible tells us He was a Man acquainted with sorrows and grief—but I believe He possessed *all* the glorious attributes in abundance, because the Bible also tells us that He came that our *joy* might be full, that we might have life abundant, which certainly includes joy. Someone has asked, "Can you imagine little children flocking around a Man who never smiled?" I believe He smiled radiantly and often. He *had* to have a great personality and magnetism to have caused those apostles to drop their work, leave all and follow Him. Human nature being what it is "in the raw," it doesn't readily respond to the glum face of a stranger. Yes, I imagine that Jesus would enjoy a Little League baseball game! Children need to feel that their Lord is with them in their play as well as in their work.

It's always a thrill to hear Dusty pray, "Help me with my arithmetic and make me a better boy and a better Christian." Sandy has said on several occasions, "Mom, when I grow up I'm not going to smoke or drink or anything!" Reminds me of folks who say, "One of these days when I get strong enough to give up a few things, I will probably become a Christian!" One never gets strong enough to become a Christian on his own—*Christ* is the Christian's strength! I told Sandy his resolutions and "don'ts" are very nice, but the most important resolution of all is to "love the Lord, thy God, with all thy heart, all thy soul and all thy mind." If Sandy does this, his "don'ts" will just naturally take care of themselves.

People make gods out of the things they "don't do"—smoking, gambling, dancing, etc.—but what about the sins of the disposition, the intents of the heart, the little, mean thoughts that no one knows about except God and us? While I, for instance, am not a tobacco fan, I rather imagine some of the great Christian saints of all time, the martyrs, had their little weaknesses in that direction, or some other. But to judge a person's standing with God on the basis that he either does or doesn't smoke or dance seems like pretty shallow thinking to me. Jesus said, "Judge not, that ye be not judged." As the Christian matures, he will put away "childish things."

Tom, I want these children to *enjoy* Jesus, and to *like* Him as a person; to feel free to confide in Him, share their joys as well as their troubles with Him. Dodie will say to me, as we are driving to the market, "Mama, Jesus and God are right in this car, is they?" I will assure her, and then she will say, "They are in the back seat, too, huh?" I have explained that God, Jesus, and the Holy Spirit are one and the same. This is a crude illustration, but I told all the children that the Holy Trinity was Three in One—and that if I had an apple and divided it into three parts, all the parts would still be one apple. In other words, one God in three parts; that Jesus is the part that wore human flesh, such as we do, and atoned for our sins; God is the Spirit, our Father; and the Holy Spirit is that still, small voice of the heart that tells us to be good and inspires us to do things for God, which makes us supremely happy. The Trinity was a complete enigma to me for years, and there are those who will question my explanation. This is simply what I believe, and our children seem to take it in their stride.

Another thing I believe to be important is for the children to see God in nature. Not long ago, Dodie and I were walking through the hills and rocks on our place, on one of the hikes she so dearly loves. She is rightly named "Little Doe," because she is just as sure-footed as a deer. It was quite windy, and Dodie started to complain that the wind was blowing her hair too much. I told her, "That's God's wind, Dodie—look, reach up and catch it; it's fun!" From then on she was captivated by it, and every time the breeze started, she would put up her arms as though to embrace it! I told her the wind sweeps away lots of dirt and cobwebs off the flowers and leaves, whips a sailboat into action, turns a windmill, and even makes pretty music, if you will take time to listen closely.

Yesterday she was scribbling on a piece of typewriter paper here on my night-stand. I asked her what she was "writing." She said, "Homework!" She then showed me her "lesson" and said, "Mama, do homework say anything?" This struck a chord within me, and I silently asked myself, "Does *my* homework with these children say anything to the world outside? Are we parents doing any homework at all with our children, in the realm of Christian-American training?" With an increased juvenile crime rate, we parents had better start "digging" and "cramming" with our children on the subject of Christian living, if we are to pass the inevitable test of standing up for Jesus at any cost!

Lovingly yours,
Mother.

Dear Tom

I am 18,000 feet high over the Texas plains, winging my way back to California after a delightful Texas visit. They crowned me "Queen of the Uvalde, Texas, Centennial" last Thursday evening at the Uvalde Stadium!

I stayed with Aunt Annie Merle Pulliam one day at the ranch, and the next at her house in town. It was a wonderful and nostalgic experience to go back to the house where I was born, on the old Fort Clark Road, where Granddaddy and Grandmother Wood raised eight fine children in the nurture and admonition of the Lord. The present occupants allowed Aunt Annie and me to go through the house—and how many memories rushed my mind! The old windmill in back of the house was merrily singing, and I remembered how my brother, Hillman, and I loved climbing it—and how, grasping a hollow iron tube, strung on the tight-wire from the platform to the garden gate, I would swing down from the platform. The old back porch was still there, where "Mama Wood," our grandmother, churned the milk every morning as she read her *Baptist Standard* and sang hymns. . . . The fireplace, where Granddaddy used to pop corn at night, read the Bible and have family prayer, and insist that all the children and grandchildren eat an orange or apple with him at bedtime. . . . The long sleeping porch, where I used to watch the huge, twinkling stars in the clear Texas sky, and listen to the Mexican folks serenading with their beautiful, haunting songs and soft strumming guitars. . . . The large dining room, where the big, happy family enjoyed old-fashioned, home-cooked meals in wonderful fellowship and quiet respect for my grandparents—for Granddaddy Wood was truly the head of the house, and the "head of the wife," as Christ is the Head of the church. When Granddaddy spoke to the children, there was no arguing over his command! It was simply understood that he was to be obeyed, and that he deserved obedience because the Bible said so—and because he believed in the Bible and practiced his Christianity every day. No one ever thought of questioning his authority—and, Tom, every one of his children revere him and my grandmother to this day. I have heard Mom say many times, "Papa was strict, but how I thank him and Mama for the training they gave us."

In sharp contrast to the above, last night Mom, Aunt Faye, and I went to see the two, much-discussed James Dean pictures, "East of Eden" and "Rebel Without a Cause." I went because Cheryl and Marion asked me to see the pictures, and how glad I am that I went! The subject matter has been rather controversial among many thoughtful people because of its explosive nature—delinquent youth. It is striking that the only two big pictures made by this late actor of such unusual talent and appeal to all ages should have dealt with this subject. God works in mysterious ways, and I believe this particular "programming" and perfect timing shows the fine hand of God.

Although the time of the first story was 1917, and the second, 1955, the problem was the same in both stories. The problem, in a nutshell, was the lack of love and the understanding of the nature of love on the part of the parents. I came away from that theater with a feeling of parental responsibility that I will not quickly forget, if ever! When Cheryl and Marion first told me parts of the "hot rod" sequences, I was aghast and indignant at such material being shown to our already mixed-up youth and I questioned the advisability of such a picture. However, they both said "every parent should see it. . . ." Now I know why. It is a *must* for parents, regardless of their feelings about motion pictures, for these two pictures reveal the necessity of *love*, for *survival*. Love is the fulfilling of the law—God's law and man's law. Love is all-encompassing. Love demands understanding, discipline, mercy, truth, justice, faith, hope, and charity. Charity, or love, says the New Testament, is the greatest of the commandments. ". . . though I give my body to be burned, and have not charity, it profiteth me nothing." In "East of Eden," the father was a deeply religious man who read his Bible constantly, who had faith and hope—but lacked true charity. He despised his wife's "weakness of character," sought to possess her in thought, word and deed, to make her conform to his own image. He really loved his own self-righteousness instead of his wife, and she left him for a life of flagrant sin, at the same time deserting their two little sons. The older boy grew to be like his mother in his way, and the father inwardly despised the boy and despised himself for ever having loved the mother. The younger boy was truly the father's son and was the obvious favorite, because in him the father saw himself. The older boy was a frantic, vulnerable soul, who ached for love and understanding from his father, and got into all kinds of trouble unwittingly, trying to win his love. The younger boy was "smug as a bug in a rug," secure in the knowledge that he was approved and cherished. By the refusal of the father charitably to understand the older boy, the younger boy's life was jealously wrecked by the older, and finally the father suffered a stroke before he recognized his mistake and gave his eldest son a chance at his love.

In "Rebel Without a Cause," the parents were truly delinquent of their responsibility of love to their children, and the children suffered miserably. The father and mother were too busy with their own pursuits to meet the psychological needs of the children. When Jim asked his father if it was necessary to participate in a dangerous game of challenge in order to prove himself a man, the father dodged the issue and talked in abstractions such as, "These things will seem silly when you are older"—without really facing up to asking the boy if it involved the danger of loss of life, or even asking him what the game was. The father was *afraid* to ask, because he did not want the responsibility of giving an answer, and he had never gained the confidence of his son. After the tragedy of the "chicken game," the boy's inherent sense of honesty demanded that he tell the police what had happened. The rest of the pathetic teen-age participants had scattered like quail after the horrible crash, but Jim, whose pitiable crime in the affair was trying to "be a man" by responding to the taunting challenge of "chicken," wanted to make a clean breast of things. His mother wrongly counseled him to "keep quiet" and not disgrace the family. The boy turned to his father and demanded allegiance to right, straight thinking. The father again shrank before the prospect of a soul-searching decision, and more tragedy occurred. It was no credit to either parent that the boy finally proved to be a hero. It was due to his own innate sense of responsibility to his fellow man. Needless to say, God was *not* the center of any of the homes represented; that fact is obvious. The children were searching for love and all that it implies; and God is love. The parents had given them everything but themselves—and the children were still hungry. When a child is hungry, he searches for appeasement, and real, honest-to-goodness Christian love is the only thing that will truly satisfy the human soul. When will we parents awake to the fact that we must *love* our children and teach them the real meaning of love—not just the self-gratification kind, but the self-sacrificial kind, by the giving of ourselves, and the giving of themselves? I dare say that there isn't a home in America that wouldn't be stirred into positive, right action by seeing these pictures.

It is to the self-sacrificial nature of our forefathers that we owe our blessed American heritage. It was the self-sacrificial giving of Abraham, Moses, John the Baptist, our blessed Lord Jesus Christ, and the disciples that enabled us to know the Revelation of God to man. And it is parents' sacrificial giving of themselves to their children, in teaching them the love of God, that will save the world. If I seem to be preaching, Tom, it is mostly to myself. God help me to be a more loving and better Christian parent!

Our little "Korean-American flower" may be here shortly. Little Debbie's first impressions of her new family are tremendously important. I believe it will be best not to overwhelm her with the whole family at the airport. Perhaps it is best for Roy and me to meet her alone, and bring her home to the children. We may take Dodie and let her escort her little sister home. I'm not sure yet. We'll have to pray about it, because this little soul is facing a rather "large newness of life," and it must be done right. Dodie is very anxious for Debbie to arrive, because the other night, during prayer time, she said, "God, make that man bring my little sister over here soon!"

As I told Mom this morning, "Raising children is serious business!" We never realize to what extent our words and actions affect the lives of our children. I feel it is all-important to stress to our children the fact that we are not perfect, but that we are trying, by the grace of God, to do the best we can for them, and we need their prayers as much as they need ours.

Lovingly yours,
Mother.

Dear Tam

Yesterday Dusty and I had quite a conference on the subject of "Truth versus Untruth"—or in plain words, the advantage of truth over lies. Children often develop the pattern of "fibbing" to avoid unpleasantness over a misdeed. The word "misdeed" is apropos, because it signifies misdoing the right thing. We have a light fixture over our kitchen table that is made of a real rolling pin. (This is not symbolic of the kitchen atmosphere, however!) Well, it seems one of the ends of the rolling pin disappeared, as did a round knob atop my prized grandfather's clock. Of course, *no one* knew a thing about it! Children have very "convenient forgetters." Dodie is too small to reach them and so is Sandy. When I questioned Dusty about it, he had a very defiant attitude, and was rather sullen. Having known Dusty for quite a spell, there is something about his countenance that usually reveals the veracity of his statements. I told him he would not be punished if he told me the truth, and he knows that I keep my promises. I believe in that, because it is important to a child's faith in the word of his parent.

I told him that our Lord said the devil is the father of lies, and when we lie we are serving the devil instead of our Lord, because our Lord is Truth, personified. No matter if no one on earth knows our misdeeds, our Heavenly Father is watching our every move, and even our thoughts. Therefore, we are never really "putting over" anything.

The expression on Dusty's face started to soften. I told him the story of George Washington, the axe and the cherry tree—how our first President started a good habit of telling the truth when he was just a boy, even though it might involve "painful consequences" for a short while. Truth is always great, and truth lives forever, because it is real. Lies finally die an ignominious death because they are not real. The people who have made our country great were people of truth and courage, who were not afraid, after having done all, to *stand* for the truth. I told Dusty that character is made up of *small* things, and it is all-important to tell the truth about small, seemingly unimportant happenings. I explained that everything we see, hear, or do is recorded in our "storeroom mind" (the subconscious mind). We should be careful to think rightly and truthfully about each situation, before it goes to the storeroom. This is vital to mental health, because truth keeps our mental storeroom clean and lies make it dirty. When we have to answer a hard question involving us personally, the "front mind" needs help, so the storeroom comes to the rescue with one of the stored answers. It is important that the storeroom be full of truths, because if that be the case, both minds will be clean and healthy; and since the mind telegraphs messages to the body, telling the truth will help our bodies, too. Jesus said, "Now ye are clean through the word which I have spoken unto you"—Jesus is Truth, and He spoke truth to His disciples, and they wrote His words of truth down for us. Jesus is really saying that we are made clean by speaking truth; because when we speak truth, He is speaking through us because He is Truth. The whole world is groaning under a heavy load of lies of all kinds. The truth makes us free. *We must not fail* to instill into our children the love of truth.

Dusty *still* says he did not take the knob on the rolling pin! Nevertheless, the situation gave me an excellent chance to speak the Word.

Lovingly yours,
Mother.

Dear Tom

This seems to be my year for illnesses, small and large! We are again shooting our television series, and I have a bad case of laryngitis. Maybe I have been using my voice too much on inconsequential things. Sandy also has a light affliction, a skin irritation that caused a swelling on the right side of his face. Both Sandy and Dodie are out here on location today at Iverson Ranch—one is asleep in Roy's station wagon and one in my car.

How I love working on location, in God's great outdoors! The spring flowers are profuse with color, and birds are outdoing themselves today with beautiful, melodic variations. How good is God! How benevolent to man! Here in front of me is a strange paradox—a huge cactus tree practically growing into a heavily-laden orange tree. One produces fruit sweet to the taste, the other, thorns, but also a strange-tasting little, round, purplish fruit that is edible and, I understand, very satisfying once you get through the hard shell.

Isn't that like life? We indulge in our pleasures very quickly, and they are, indeed, sweet to the taste, but also quickly forgotten, for the partaking is easy. Our "thorny" experiences we long remember because the partaking of them is often difficult and painful before we reach the "peaceable fruit of righteousness" and understanding. Yet both are beautiful and created by the same God. Therefore, ought we not to be thankful for both?

Sunday, Reverend Hayward, at the Chatsworth Community Methodist Church, talked about "packing our bags" for our journey to heaven. He said every day of our lives we are packing our bags—and many of the items will be useless there. I thought about that a lot during the past week. For an experiment, I have tried to remember at the end of each day what items I had packed during the day—and you know, it was a little discouraging. Even our *thoughts* will be in the bag! We can't help ugly thoughts presenting themselves to our minds, but it is our privilege to take them in or to turn them away—and it is surprising how they nag at us for entrance! Once they are in, they are very hard to evict. And I might add, they make terrible tenants because they create nothing but confusion. Who was it who said, "You can't prevent crows from flying over your head, but you can stop them from building nests in your hair"? I like that, and wish I could remember it oftener.

Yesterday we got word that our little Lee (Debbie to us) will arrive from Korea at 8:15 A.M. next Tuesday at International Airport. Our shooting schedule is very tight for that day, so we we are trying to work out an arrangement for Roy to be picked up at the studio by helicopter and flown to the airport to meet the Pan-American flight. I will drive there with Dodie in my car, because we think it important for Dodie, being the baby of the family, to welcome the "new youngest Rogers," even if there *are* only four months difference in age. This is always a delicate matter. We plan to let Dodie shake hands with her first. Then, as I have to go back to the studio, we will take both little girls with us for the day and let them get acquainted before we take the new one to her new San Fernando Valley home. We hope she will be happy with us, because she will have a difficult adjustment. All the children are very excited about her coming and have been anxiously awaiting the arrival date.

Someone remarked not long ago, "You people have quite an international family." Well, we pray the Lord will help us prove that God's family *is* international, and that it is possible to live in love and harmony, as brothers and sisters, despite different backgrounds. There are other families who have done it and we believe, the Lord willing, that we can do it too. If a family can do this under one roof, why can't the whole world family do it? We believe peace starts in the heart of the individual, reaches out to the family, to the community, to the nation—and from there to other nations. Peace stems from love, and love is the fulfilling of God's law. *Right* is might. However, might is not always right—but love *is*!

Lovingly yours,
Mother.

Dear Tom

Tom, this poor, weary, old world lost another little angel of light this week—little Nancy Hamilton died Thursday morning. Blessed little Nancy, who helped countless people to forget their problems because she bore her heavy affliction with such grace, and turned desperate thoughts Godward. She always wanted a pair of red shoes—but she had no feet to wear them. When they finally had to amputate one of her deformed legs, her mother bought the red shoes, thinking she might wear them on the artificial legs they hoped to put on Nancy so she could walk. But, like little Robin, Nancy was destined to fly! Instead of red shoes, she got wings.

Linda and I went over to Santa Monica today to say our last goodbye to this child of God who blessed our entire household during her unusual ministry in this vale of tears. Nancy and Linda were very close. It was Linda who first invited Nancy and her mother into our house in Hollywood, as they were taking a stroll in the neighborhood one day. From that day on, we felt that Nancy Hamilton and her courageous mother were part of our family. Nancy and her mother lived far above her pitiful physical condition for all of Nancy's fourteen years. This child wanted no sympathy for her handicap—she wanted to help others. And help she did! She certainly helped me.

Nancy fulfilled her mission in a glorious way. Only Eternity will reveal the scope of God's work through her. The Bible says there remains a rest for the people of God. I know Nancy is enjoying the restful fruit of her labors.

Lovingly yours,
Mother.

Dear Tom

So much has transpired the past week that I hardly know where to start this letter. Last Tuesday, little Debbie Lee arrived on "Operation Stork," via Pan-American Air Lines, through the auspices of Dr. Bob Pierce and World Vision, Inc. Cheryl, Linda, Marion, Dodie, Roy and I left Chatsworth practically at dawn, in order to stop by the house of our make-up man in Westwood, as it was en route to the airport and we had to go directly to the studio after picking up our new daughter. The plane was a few minutes late and what a thrill of anticipation! All the prospective parents were literally "champing at the bit," waiting for their "sight-unseen children"! I was so excited as that plane door opened that I caught myself jumping up and down and crying at the same time! Dr. Pierce stepped down with Debbie Lee in his arms, followed by the other children and helpers. There were newsreels and photographers everywhere—and what happy confusion there was as the parents all pressed forward for their new children.

Little Debbie came right to me in a very composed and dignified manner. She is even prettier than her pictures. She did not smile, but accepted us very calmly and matter-of-factly. We took all the girls right to the studio, as the crew was waiting to shoot our first scene of the day. On the way down, I held Debbie on my lap, while Dodie made the first friendly overtures. Debbie was quite reserved, and sort of clung to me as Dodie would attempt to take her hand. I tried not to force anything, as a first meeting is very important with children. By the time we reached the studio, Debbie was evincing interest in everything about her and offering comments in Korean. Everyone seemed quite taken by her and the day was wonderful! At lunch, Debbie surprised us with her excellent table manners. Eating is a serious business with this young lady, and she really "falls to," as they say in the West.

However, when we got home and I started to put her to bed, she showed the first resistance—she wanted no part of it and was quite vociferous in her dislike of a bed. Finally, Dodie gave her "Ethel," a blond, blue-eyed doll, and Debbie consented to explore the Land of Nod. She repeated a little prayer after me perfectly, and after assuring Dodie that I still loved her (oh, yes, the green-eyed monster was rousing itself already!), I prepared for bed myself. Linda is "house mother" to the two little girls, and a good mother she will make some day.

Early the next morning, I tiptoed into their big room, and all three were awake. Linda informed me that Debbie had crawled out of bed four times and preferred sleeping on the floor. I have since learned that this is the custom in Korea, only Korean floors are heated and ours are cold! We have put Dusty's old bed rails on her bed, with a heavy bookcase at the foot, trying to keep her from climbing out in the middle of the night!

She is really a delightful and winsome child, and very affectionate. I have become "Mama" very quickly to her, and already it seems she has always been here. This child adjusts beautifully. Dodie is alternately overjoyed and jealous. Each time Dodie feels slighted because of any attention to the new youngster, I remind her that she begged for a "little sister." The real adjustment, I think, is always made by the child or children already established in the home, who might be prone to feel displaced.

However, I am happy to report that things have settled down, and Dodie quite often says, "Mama, Debbie cute!" Yesterday they were playing and Dodie, rather exasperated at one of Debbie's antics, stood with her hands on her hips and said, "Mama, her just like a little kid!" Dodie is quite the big sister. Oddly enough, though one is Indian and the other Korean, they look very much alike. When I see them playing happily with radiant smiles, I am so grateful to the Lord for the privilege of housing these little "orphans of the storm."

Debbie is fearful of dogs, and when Joaquin, our big Weimaraner, tried to befriend her, she nearly went into hysterics. It has since been explained that, during the Korean conflict, many of their stray dogs were eaten, and the only dogs left are powerful, well-trained and vicious watchdogs. The children are taught to fear them, and it has taken lots of explaining and petting Joaquin in front of Debbie, before she will even look at him without cringing.

We are having a wonderful time up here atop Big Bear Mountain. Several of our television pictures concern boating and fishing, so we thought it would be a good chance to bring the children here for a vacation, while "Pa" and I worked. Betty and James Ordono, our house couple, came with us, and we are occupying a lovely big lake cottage.

Somehow, God seems so close here among the tall, whispering pine trees, the incredibly blue sky, the bright stars that seem so near, the glorious sunrise and sunset. Yesterday, Dusty and Sandy took me fishing out on the lake, and we caught *fifty* little blue-gill fish. Dusty manned the motor and made an excellent operator. We had a wonderful time. Roy had to work, so I made it up to him by frying some of the fish for his breakfast this morning at six o'clock! Afterwards, I took a stroll along the lake for about two miles, and Tom, I had a real "Christian experience." Let me tell you about it. As I was sauntering along the waterfront, I became aware of two little birds flying close over my head. I had been meditating on the goodness of God in His wonderful bounty to us, and suddenly it occurred to me that God wanted to speak to me, and I should be still. I stopped dead in my tracks and stood quietly. The two little birds flew over to a post directly in front of me and sat quietly facing me. Suddenly, they rose in the air, circled me and flew back to the fence, facing me. They did this three times—still I waited. Then, in my mind I heard these words, "Herein is my Father glorified, that ye bear much fruit." All of a sudden I realized that I must "get on the ball" with regard to witnessing to His power—that perhaps my "Martha work" was taking precedence over my "Mary work"—and then I realized that I had not been keeping up with my correspondence and my systematic Bible study. I started walking again and just as I started up a hill, two huge dogs came bounding toward me, with menacing barks. My first reaction was panic. Then I remembered: "Resist evil and he will flee from you." So I abruptly turned toward the dogs and held out a welcoming hand, entreating them to come to me. This, I figured, was facing a crisis with love instead of fear, though inside I was shaking! The dogs stopped about a foot from me, then both pounced on me, trying to lick my face.

I walked along with them for a few feet and just ahead on top of the hill, two little Boston bulldogs came into view. The two big dogs charged up the hill, barking ferociously, and it appeared by the growling that they were going to attack the little dogs. The little dogs never budged, simply stood like two little sentinels, facing us with legs rigid and hair bristling. The big dogs again ran within two feet of them and abruptly stopped, turned and ran away.

It came to me that we must *face* evil, not run from it; because when we run, evil pursues. Evil must be "stared down." Thousands are neurotic because they try to escape problems, only to face bigger ones farther down the line. This is something we need to teach our children early. Many children start such neuroses by lying to avoid unpleasant issues, and the habit becomes a malignant one.

Lovingly yours,
Mother.

Dear Tom

Our family will hate to leave Big Bear. We all love it. The children remarked that they would like to stay all summer. Somehow there is such a feeling of freedom up here. The people seem to be free of pretense, and there doesn't seem to be any of the "keep up with the Joneses" attitude. Like Popeye, of funnies fame, they present the "I yam what I yam, and that's all I yam!" This is a very comfortable atmosphere.

Speaking of putting on a front—not long ago I was discussing the importance of "being yourself" with Cheryl, Marion, and Linda. The girls often balk at suggestions about their appearance with the horrified, "Oh, Mama, I wouldn't be found dead in that. *Nobody* wears that!" Then they will adopt certain mannerisms peculiar to a certain television or movie star, or some girl they admire. So far, Linda has remained pretty much herself and I hope she continues that way. All three of the girls have great natural charm, and it's a pity to mask it by imitating the charms of another. This is a hard thing to put over with teen-agers. Only those who are all-out Christians seem to have the courage to be fearlessly honest and to shine forth in their own God-given individuality.

Dusty and Sandy have had a wonderful time fishing. Roy is associated with some fine folks up here, the Ray Sharps, in the boat-landing business—boats, fishing tackle, etc.—and the boys have certainly taken to it as ducks take to water. Speaking of water, yesterday as I stood on the edge of Big Bear Lake, at Gray's Landing, looking across the wind-rippling blue water, a wonderful peace enveloped me. I was reminded of the fine sermon on "regeneration" we heard at Big Bear Community Church at the eleven o'clock service. The pastor was referring to the necessity of being "born of water *and* the spirit." He said he believed the "water" represented our physical birth and the "spirit" meant the birth of a new life through placing our faith in Christ. Water has real therapeutic value in the treatment of nervous ailments. It is difficult to be tense and worried when you are in the water, or on it in a boat, or even gazing upon it from the shore. Most children revel in their baths. Water is so necessary to earthly existence. People are prone to forget the benefits of water until they are without it, and then they pray for it. The Scriptures say that the Spirit of God *moved* upon the face of the waters. Here, at the very *beginning*, is water and the Spirit, and all through the course of history, both have been vital. We must encourage our children to like water, for it is healthful.

A friend said to me, "When I look upon the water, my

mind becomes almost a blank, and I am so relaxed." This is reversion to babyhood, for a baby is born of water, with a clean, new, blank and relaxed mind—and frankly, I think we all need to experience this often. Our minds become too cluttered.

At dusk yesterday, the boys and I took a two-mile walk together. The pine-scented air is so crisp, and it felt good to take long strides and deep breaths. When we got home, I took a warm bath and a quick "to-bed," for Roy and I had early calls this morning; his was practically a "dawn call."

You know, Tom, that walk was real fun—good exercise, and a chance for easy companionship with the children. The boys chatted about many extremely interesting things. I thoroughly enjoyed it and so did they. At times like this you really can get close to your children. Families not only should *pray* together, they should *play* together and work together in common tasks. When you become a child in play with your children, they are not afraid to venture certain confidences and bits of newly-gained knowledge, because you are one with them at play. Instead of being their taskmaster, you are playmate. How Jesus loved little children!

I can't imagine Him ever being shocked at their antics. He understood them, but He also believed in the obedience of children to their parents. He obeyed His parents and was even "obedient unto death" to His Heavenly Father. Reverend Hayward, at our Chatsworth Church, said to parents that their *nay* should be *nay*, and their *yea* should be *yea* to their children, for a child needs to feel that the word of his parents is solid. This means psychological security to the child. Humans who obey no one usually destroy others and in the end destroy themselves. It is so much better to learn obedience early in life! The chastisement hurts worse in the later years.

I have talked to parents who were fearful of punishing, particularly of spanking, an adopted child. I believe they do the child an injustice, for the child needs to know the boundaries of conduct. After all, we are all the adopted children of God through Christ, and God, our Father, doesn't hesitate to scourge us. The Bible says, "He scourgeth every son whom He receiveth." Otherwise, we are not really sons at all but illegitimate children, according to God's Holy Word. Therefore, ought we not to give an adopted child the same careful instruction that we give our natural children? God spared not His own Son, so why should He spare us, the adopted ones? Ought we not to absorb this example in the case of an adopted child? In Proverbs 22:15 I read, "Foolishness is bound in the heart of a child; but the rod of correction shall drive it far from him."

Lovingly yours,
Mother.

Dear Tom

Here we are at Forest Home Retreat with the Hollywood Christian Group—high up in the mountains for a two-day retreat, to be quiet and to be wisely counseled in the things of Christ for a time of real refreshment in Him, who is the Eternal Fountain of Life. Our meeting started with lunch at 12:30 in the clubhouse dining room, followed by a devotional from that dear, Christian lady, Miss Henrietta Mears, a veritable powerhouse of the Spirit of Christ. How she challenged us! I came up here dreadfully tired, Tom, needing spiritual and physical refreshment badly, and Miss Mears' talk was a terrific vitamin shot. Before she started her devotional on "Are you growing in your Christian life?", I was approached by a counselor for the Forest Home staff of young people serving during the conference down the hill, to give a short witness at 7:15 tonight, just before our song-fest and night meeting starts. My emotions told me to say, "No, I am too tired and I need every minute of this retreat to refuel!" But somehow, I couldn't say no, and when Miss Mears had finished, I knew why. Witnessing is part of Christian growth.

It was impossible for Roy to come with me this year because of his heavy schedule, and I will have to absorb enough to take back to him and the children! Jack O'Shea, Frances and Joy Eilers and Joy's house guest from Westminster Choir School, at Princeton, drove up with me.

Miss Mears told of her mother's mighty Christian influence on her life, how she let Christ live in and through her. She said that when her mother passed on into the presence of our Lord, people said she was the most perfect person in sinful human flesh that they had ever known. She said her mother had quite a temper as a child, and when she gave herself to the Lord Jesus Christ, she earnestly pleaded with Him to help her get rid of that temper. Miss Mears' father said that not once had he ever heard her raise her voice in harshness or anger and that every time she got a chance to tell anyone about the Lord, she did it. What a testimony, and what a heritage for Miss Mears! Miss Mears said that when her mother died, Miss Mears prayed God to give her some of her mother's power in Christ. I know God heard Miss Mears, for she is such a radiant, spiritual dynamo that just to be in her presence is to feel the vibrations.

Oh, how I pray for godly patience with our children. "A soft answer turneth away wrath"—and how many times I bark! Of course, I bark more than I bite, as what parent doesn't! But barking is jarring to the nerves. More of realizing the presence of our Master, or a constant attitude of prayer would eliminate this, and so

I am going consciously to try to "play the game of minutes," as suggested by Dr. Frank Laubach, as an aid to a closer walk with Jesus. In other words, as the Bible says, "He will keep him in perfect peace whose mind is stayed on thee." I will try consciously to keep my mind on Christ as much as possible. When the mind is concentrating on Christ and His goodness, it does not direct the tongue into a harsh, corroding tone.

I believe most mothers, deep down, long to be gentle. Only by abiding in Christ is that attribute gained. That is one of the fruits of the spirit. Jesus said, "Abide in me." Without our abiding in the True Vine, our fruit will be nil. "By their fruits, ye shall know them." Lord, help me to bear much fruit. Tom, I am sure that is what my experience with the two birds meant—that I have not been *abiding* in Christ, but in myself.

Christendom lost a mighty warrior when Dawes Trotman gave his life to save a drowning girl this week. As our Master said concerning great loves, Dawes laid down his life for his friends. Miss Mears attended his funeral and said it was no funeral; it was a testimony to the victory over death, in Christ. His wife spoke at the funeral; her eyes were clear and shining with Christian assurance.

The other day I heard the story of a hungry, seeking soul who was invited to dinner in the home of a professing Christian family. This woman had received Christian witness and was hoping to see true Christianity in action in this family. At the dinner table, each member offered a beautiful prayer of thanks, but as soon as the prayers were over, the children started arguing in loud voices, the parents shouting them down; and their Christian witness was automatically canceled out in the eyes of the visitor. "What you are stands over you—and thunders so that I cannot hear what you say. . . ." When I heard this story, my face grew very red, remembering some of our "hashing" at the table. And when I signed the register at Forest Home, I prayed the Lord to give me more patience and a soft answer, when pandemonium breaks loose.

It has now been one week since the Forest Home Retreat, and looking back over the last few days, I have discovered the Lord has really been helping me to keep calm in stress. Of course, a few times I "looked away" and started barking orders like a top sergeant, but at least He gave me the grace to realize it at the time, and to soften my voice in explanation to the children. You know, the more you really want to know the Lord and walk by faith in Him, the more glaring are your faults. The Bible says, "There is nothing hidden that shall not be revealed." Tom, I never realized how utterly dependent we are on God until I really desired to be what He wanted me to be. Now I know that we are nothing without His grace.

It was so wonderful to have you and Barbara, Mindy and Candy here last night, and especially to have you and Barbara attend the meeting of the Hollywood Christian Group here at the ranch. Guess we must have had about 150 people in our living room, dining room, and front porch. My heart was very full when you and Barb, Cheryl, Marion and Linda sang, "Sweet Hour of Prayer" in the program, just before our speaker, Dr.

Hayward, asked, "Just how big is your God?" He said we are no bigger than our God—when God is really big to us, miracles happen in our lives. Children find no problem in accepting the supernatural, because God is *big* to them and can accomplish the impossible. Oh! If we would remain childlike in our awe of God, how different our lives would be. We try to relegate God to our smallness, and then wonder why we suffer defeat in our Christian experience. *God is All* and in all! If we could just remember that in our dealings with others.

Little Candy looked thin to me today, but our God is able to strengthen her, Tom. He is her strength and her portion. When I held her on my lap, with her fragrant little brown curls against my cheek, it was like holding Robin again. . . . Candy's smile brings back wonderful memories of my little angel. They were not afflicted in the same way, but they have the same unearthly sweetness of smile in their eyes. Candy's weakness will strengthen you and Barbara, and God is, all the while, holding and supporting her in the hollow of His hand. How gracious God was to give both your little girls an exceptional musical talent. The songs from the hearts of your children will help to ease your burdens.

Today is the Lord's Day again, and a beautiful day it is! We had a wonderful Sunday school lesson, the second chapter of I John, and then a fine sermon on setting a goal in life and working toward it, in Christ. It was brought out that our Lord Jesus had one goal, to bring the kingdom of God to human beings, and even seeing the cross loom ahead failed to stop Him. To have a goal is so vital to life—and of course, the ultimate goal of every soul should be to achieve full stature in Christ, regardless of our vocation. The vocation should be the means, not the end.

What a glorious vocation is parenthood! Oh, that parents everywhere would awaken to the potential joy of fulfillment in the lives of their children! The child learns something through each experience, and so does the parent. We really relive our childhood through the lives of our children—and it is always well for us to remember, in dealing with our children, that we must see through their eyes as well as our own.

Lovingly yours,
Mother.

Dear Tom

Perhaps I am a little stern on the "fibbing" issue. But, on the other hand, our Lord exalted *truth,* for He said He is Truth—and if a child gets in the habit of fibbing, how can he enjoy fellowship with Jesus?

For instance, Sandy is going to summer school at the military academy. While he was dressing for school last week, I noticed he put on bathing trunks under his jeans in place of regular "boy's briefs." I knew there was swimming at school, and told him to take off the bathing trunks and carry them in a towel. He protested vehemently, saying, "They *told* me to wear my bathing suit under my jeans." This didn't sound right to me, but I took him at his word, feeling that he surely would have time to dry his trunks around the pool before donning his jeans again. The result was that he contracted a chest cold which kept him out of school for nearly a week. When I called his teacher, she was aghast at the fib he had told about the bathing trunks, for each child had been carefully instructed to bring the trunks in a bath towel. Yes, you guessed it—Sandy was shirking the responsibility of carrying the trunks and towel to and from school. Because he lied to me, several things happened to him. He had to take a penicillin shot, aspirin for high fever, and miss all swimming for about ten days. He will not be allowed to swim at school, only at home. The time he used for swimming at school will now be used for a nap, to rebuild the damage to his body caused by the cold, which might have been avoided had he obeyed instructions.

Another instance: Debbie, our Korean lass, was supposed to be napping on Friday. Instead, she was quietly getting into difficulty! She found a bobby pin on the floor, and attempted to stick it in a double socket electric wall outlet. She stuck one end of the bobby pin in the top part and the other end in the bottom part, the current instantly heating the pin to white heat and burning three of her fingers. The Lord was merciful in His protection, because she could have had wet hands and been killed on the spot. Debbie learned a lesson in obedience and to respect electricity. Had she obeyed instructions, her fingers would have been relaxed in restful sleep, rather than smarting and burning under awkward bandages for two days.

Today at Sunday school, Marion, our Scottish lass, was assisting the regular teacher in Junior class. She reported that Dusty and Sandy were a "couple of bad actors" all during class, being no end of harassment to the teacher. There was much giggling, punching and general "horsing around" during a story example about an apartment fire. It seems that when the teacher explained that the victims were badly burned, Sandy piped up to one of his roguish side-kicks, "Oh, my bottom is burning now!" Believe me, Tom, *I* would have burned *his* bottom with a stick, if Marion had just called me from my class! Dusty was a bit more artful in his misbehavior, but had to be called on the carpet by the principal, along with two or three other boys.

The result: They are both spending Sunday afternoon in their pajamas in bed in their respective rooms, quietly meditating the advisability of behaving in God's house, instead of being out in the hills in their usual Sunday afternoon manner. I told them that they must have been very tired and nervous to behave in such unseemly fashion in God's house . . . therefore, rest would help them to calm down. It was very difficult to keep a straight face when Marion told me about Sandy's "burning"—but of course I had to let him see that he had profoundly shocked and disappointed his mother.

You sometimes wonder if you are "getting through" at all to your children, and then, at the most unexpected times, they will delight and astonish you with their accumulation of wisdom. These wonderful moments more than make up for the hours of seemingly futile effort on the part of parents to "train up a child in the way he should go."

I have just been asked to quote seven favorite scriptures of Holy Writ, and to state why they are favorites. Here they are:

Proverbs 22:6—"Train up a child in the way he should go: and when he is old, he will not depart from it." To train up a child in the way is the greatest gift a parent can bestow, because Jesus Christ is the Way, and in Jesus Christ the child finds life abundant, purposeful, challenging, and victorious.

John 3:16—"For God so loved the world, that he gave his only begotten Son, that whosoever believeth in him should not perish, but have everlasting life." God so loved us that He bestowed upon us the supreme gift, His Son, to live and die for us, so that we might live eternally through His sacrifice. I do not understand a love this great, but I accept it joyfully and gratefully—and through receiving this gift, my life has been wonderfully transformed.

John 11:25—"Jesus said unto her, I am the resurrection, and the life: he that believeth in me, though he were dead, yet shall he live." What a glorious promise! For the true Christian, death holds no terror, but rather anticipation of life in a larger and more wonderful way.

John 14:6—"Jesus saith unto him, I am the way, the truth, and the life: no man cometh unto the Father, but by me." This is a very definite statement concerning the way of life. It is satisfying and reassuring to know that we do not have to depend on ourselves to grope our way toward heaven. We give ourselves to Him, Jesus Christ, and He is our Way. He will live through us, and we can be sure we are in and on the way to heaven.

II Chronicles 7:14—"If my people, which are called by my name, shall humble themselves, and pray, and seek my face, and turn from their wicked ways; then will I hear from heaven, and will forgive their sin, and will heal their land." America is called by His name—

a "Christian nation." God is too pure to behold iniquity, according to the Bible. He turns His face away from it. The sin of materialism separates us from God and causes all kinds of trouble. True healing is first of the soul, and then works outward. Only God can really heal the soul. If America will put God first, all things necessary to our well-being will be added, just as the Bible promises.

I Samuel 16:7—"But the Lord said unto Samuel, Look not on his countenance, or on the height of his stature; because I have refused him: for the Lord seeth not as man seeth; for man looketh on the outward appearance, but the Lord looketh on the heart." God judges the motive before the deed. This is why we are not truly capable of judging others. Man is unable to probe the heart of another man. This, I believe, is why Jesus told us to forgive not only seven times, but "seventy times seven," and let God do the judging.

Colossians 3:20—"Children, obey your parents in all things: for this is well pleasing unto the Lord." This passage needs no explanation. It is a simple, stated fact that God loves and demands obedience. In the school of life, parents can be likened to teachers of elementary school—if the children are not well-grounded in loving and careful discipline and a sense of responsibility, when they reach the high school of life they are apt to flunk their grades, because the Supreme Teacher has irrevocable rules and is no respecter of students when it comes to grading exams.

Lovingly yours,
Mother.

Dear Tom

This week we received a request for a letter on total abstinence for the Michigan Federation of Youth Temperance Council. We get many inquiries on the liquor problem. I just finished writing them a letter in which I said:

"The greatest thing a person can do is to give himself back to God, our Creator, through the sacrifice of our Lord Jesus Christ in our behalf. St. Paul said, 'Present your bodies a living sacrifice, holy, acceptable unto God, which is our reasonable sacrifice.' "

The Bible also tells us that our bodies are the temple of the Holy Spirit. Anything that defiles the house of the Spirit must be displeasing to God, for our Lord Jesus promised He would send us "The Comforter," who would guide us into all truth. It is utterly impossible to be under the influence of liquor and the Holy Spirit at the same time. I know this, because before I gave my life to the Lord, I used to partake of liquor in what I considered was a "reasonable" way. Jesus said we cannot serve God and Mammon. We have to choose—and it is a constant choosing in our lives.

Again, St. Paul said, "Be not drunk with wine, wherein is excess, but be filled with the spirit." Not everyone can take just one drink and stop. Those who say they are able to take just one drink or two and stop must remember that they may be influencing a weaker person who is not able to control his "intake." We are told not to be stumbling blocks to our brothers and that if we offend him at meat or drink, we should abstain from it.

Why take the first drink? Liquor is not a stimulant. Rather, it is a depressant. It slows down our normal reactions, cheating the brain of its usual balance in judgment in making decisions, large or small.

It is true that liquor, at times, might have been useful in a medical way, but among medical men there seems to be some doubt about that. However, when we consider the present wanton drunkenness, broken homes, broken bodies from automobile accidents and other liquor-inspired tragedies, its medical merit pales in comparison with its destructive potentialities.

Why not choose the highest and best way to joy—the true Spirit, God's Holy Spirit? This brings true joy, wonderful purpose and peace in our lives.

Lovingly yours,
Mother.

Dear Tom

Dusty is playing a part in one of our television pictures, which is about some potential delinquents who have come for a vacation at a summer camp run by Roy. He has really done a fine job with his lines. Dusty is completely natural, just like Roy, and I think that's great! There are those who are sure Dusty will follow in his Dad's footsteps. I think Dusty will make his own footprints and I think that's the way it should be. If God's purpose for his life leads through show business, that's fine. But God made us all different, and no one can adequately fill another's shoes. The title of "Junior" is many times a handicap when Junior steps into his father's business, because he is unconsciously compared to his father, particularly if the father has had an appreciable amount of success. I want Dusty to be what his heart tells him to be, but first of all to be a Christian.

We are taking all the children to the Ohio State Fair and the Iowa State Fair. This will be a tour! However, I will breathe a lot easier if they are all with us for the two weeks, because it is very difficult to cancel out shows and go home if a child at home is sick or has an accident. When you were little and I was on tour, you were with my Mom, and I *knew* you would be all right, emotionally and physically. I think grandmothers are wonderful substitutes for mothers, but my Mom isn't well enough to handle seven children now, and neither is Roy's Mom—so Ohio and Iowa, here we come! The State Fairs will be educational as well as fun. Then we plan to drive them out to Duck Run, Ohio, where Roy spent his childhood. He wants to show them the house he and his Dad built, and the old well where they used to cool their milk and butter.

We are featuring all the children in our patriotic and Christian spot in the show. Here's what we plan to do. . . .

Introduce the children one by one and have them say the American Pledge of Allegiance, with choral response from the Sons of the Pioneers, with Roy and me singing the second verse and chorus of "America, the Beautiful." Then Roy and I will give a short talk on the importance of faith in God and spiritual education for children. Naturally, the emphasis is on Christianity because this is primarily a Christian nation, and we feel that Christianity has made our nation what it is.

Dodie "pulled one" the other day. Betty, our housekeeper, said Dodie had been very ugly to little Debbie when they were "in a hassle over some toys" in their playroom. Betty asked Dodie why she had been unkind to little Debbie. Dodie said, "I don't want her here!," whereupon Betty marched her in to talk to Mama. I told Dodie it was *her* idea to have a little sister, as Mindy had Candy, and she was reminded of the many times she demanded, "When is my little sister going to be here?" I made her kiss Debbie and tell her she was sorry, although she did it rather grudgingly. I noticed the next night during Grace at dinner that she thanked God for her little sister. Adjustments never come very easily—but they come. That's the important thing. There are many pros and cons about adopting children into a family that already has children. In defense of the latter, children who learn to adjust to an adopted brother or sister are already well on their way to success in the art of adjusting to problems of life which will come later.

Lovingly yours,
Mother.

Dear Tom

I am preparing next Sunday's lesson for the adult class, taken from the third chapter of the First Epistle of John. These are, indeed, meaty Scriptures, and very challenging to the professed Christian.

The fourth verse: "Whosoever committeth sin transgresseth also the law: for sin is the transgression of the law." One of the definitions of the word "sin" (you know, this word is very unpopular these days), is "to miss the mark." The Bible says that he that knows to do good, and does not do it, to that man it is a sin. The sin of *omission* is sometimes graver than the sin of *commission*, because by omitting a good deed some soul may be lost. The good deed might have made the recipient look Godward and influenced him to seek to know the *motivation* of the good deed, which, of course, is the Holy Spirit. There is power to generate light in a light bulb, but the switch must be turned on first. Before God gave Moses the law, man was, to some extent, ignorant of what constituted sin; but now that we have the law, man is judged by it. But, as Christians, when we transgress the law, we can be forgiven through the shed blood of our Saviour Jesus Christ. This is why He died on the cross, because He knew our flesh is carnal, and profits us nothing. He took the form of our sin and nailed it to the tree of Calvary to satisfy justice, for God is a just God as well as a merciful God. What wonderful love He had for us! We should cherish that truth in our hearts every time we hear the name of Jesus.

The fifth verse: "And ye know that he was manifested to take away our sins; and in him is no sin." Jesus said to Pilate, as He was being questioned, "For this cause came I into the world." Praise His name!

Sixth verse: "Whosoever abideth in him sinneth not: whosoever sinneth hath not seen him, neither known him." This is a very difficult passage to digest, because the sincere Christian *knows* that he is sinful by nature; but let us look farther, by the light of the Holy Spirit. The Bible tells us that we actually are two persons. The fleshly man is the natural man and is subject to the bondage of sin, and the spiritual man is born of God and abhors sin. The spiritual part of us is the "new creature in Christ Jesus," born when we accept Jesus as Saviour and Lord, by the baptism of the Holy Spirit. As we harbor ugly thoughts, such as hate, self-pride, envy, and scorn, we feed the natural man and encourage him to grow, which is the opposite of what we should do. Every wrong thought should be rejected and a good thought put in its place, thereby making more room for the Holy Spirit to abide more fully in the temple of our hearts and feeding our spiritual man. Our goal, as Christians, is finally to reach the full stature of Christ, so that we may enjoy eternity in His presence. The Bible says that flesh and blood cannot inherit the kingdom of God, that it is to be found in the realm of the Spirit—which to me explains the Scripture, ". . . whosoever sinneth hath not seen him, neither known him (Christ)." The flesh must die for the spirit to live. The Christian's life is a daily crucifixion of the flesh, if he is really to grow in spirit. In other words, we must *subject* the flesh to Christ—present our bodies a *sacrifice* to Him in our daily lives.

Now, let's look at the term "crucifixion of the flesh." Jesus said that we should *serve* each other, and He also said he who would save his life will lose it, but he that loses his life for Jesus' sake, shall find it. We can start today losing our lives for His sake—to put our fellow man before ourselves—to crucify our selfishness. For instance, when we are driving our car in a full stream of traffic, and some oncoming car wishes to turn left where there is no light—even though we have the right-of-way, we can serve the Lord by stopping and allowing that man to make his left-hand turn. Or, perhaps we are at the grocery store, being checked out with a heaping cart of groceries—someone behind us has only a few items and we can very easily take a few more seconds and invite that person to be checked out first. No, we don't *have* to do it; but when we do these things we are feeding our spiritual selves and crucifying the flesh. These are, perhaps, crude illustrations for so profound a subject, but Christianity must be lived in the small things so that it becomes a habit of practice. Psychology and psychiatry tell us that our lives are governed by habit patterns. The Christian should develop Christian habits of attitude and behavior so that he will *react* to situations in a Christlike way.

Seventh verse: "Little children, let no man deceive you: he that doeth righteousness is righteous, even as he (Jesus) is righteous." Jesus said, "By their fruits, ye shall know them." We are not justified by our works in the sight of God, but we are justified by faith in Jesus Christ. However, our *works* are the *result* of our faith, and if we really have faith, we will produce fruit, or works.

Eighth verse: "He that committeth sin is of the devil; for the devil sinneth from the beginning. For this purpose the Son of God was manifested, that he might destroy the works of the devil." Satan was responsible for the curse on our flesh when he first tempted man to disobey God. Satan asked for admittance into the heart of Adam and was admitted; the heart of man has been tormented by him ever since. David cried out, "Create in me a clean heart, O God, and renew a right spirit within me." Man has always, since the original fall, longed to have his heart restored to its first estate of joy and peace with God. Jesus did that for us on Calvary, but we must accept it to realize it.

Ninth verse: "Whosoever is born of God doth not commit sin; for his seed remaineth in him: and he cannot sin, because he is born of God." Our natural self is begotten through the flesh, but our spiritual self is begotten by God only, and the seed is the Holy Spirit. Only the Holy Spirit can *beget* another spiritual self. We cannot beget a Christian—God's Holy Spirit "borns" the new Christian. The spiritual seed is God's, not ours.

Tenth verse: "In this the children of God are manifest, and the children of the devil: whosoever doeth not righteousness is not of God, neither he that loveth not his brother." A person who lives a consistently wicked life has chosen to serve the fleshly, instead of the spiritual man. Jesus said, "Ye cannot serve God and Mammon." We must choose constantly. Love is the fulfilling of the law. If we do not love our brother, even though he might appear evil, we are serving Satan. We love the person, but hate the sin which harms him.

Eleventh verse: "For this is the message that ye heard from the beginning, that we should love one another." This is very plain.

Twelfth verse: "Not as Cain who was of that wicked one, and slew his brother. And wherefore slew he him? Because his own works were evil, and his brother's righteous." We've all heard people who love to criticize the smallest misdemeanor of another, and particularly the failings of a Christian. This builds up their ego, because secretly they realize that the Christian has something they do not have, and it makes them feel insecure. If they can tear down the good report of the other person they feel they "aren't so bad, after all."

Thirteenth, fourteenth, and fifteenth verses: "Marvel not, my brethren, if the world hate you. We know that we have passed from death unto life, because we love the brethren. He that loveth not his brother abideth in death. Whosoever hateth his brother is a murderer: and ye know that no murderer hath eternal life abiding in him." The Bible says the "whole world lieth in the arms of the wicked one." When we, as Christians, face violent opposition to our faith and works, we should remember this and pray for our persecutors. We must overcome evil with good. A real Christian will not hate anyone, because hate is destructive, and the Holy Spirit of God abiding in the heart will strive to overcome the situation with love. He who really hates is quite capable of killing. Death is the enemy of life, and Jesus is Life. Therefore, the man who harbors hate is abiding in death instead of in life.

Sixteenth, seventeenth, eighteenth and nineteenth verses: "Hereby perceive we the love of God, because he laid down his life for us: and we ought to lay down our lives for the brethren. But whoso hath this world's good, and seeth his brother have need, and shutteth up his bowels of compassion from him, how dwelleth the love of God in him? My little children, let us not love in word, neither in tongue; but in deed and in truth. And hereby we know that we are of the truth, and shall assure our hearts before him." If our love is in lip service only, we are deceiving ourselves. If we know to do a deed for the Lord and talk about it only, then our hearts will condemn us—but if we follow through, our hearts will be warmed and assured of His grace and truth in our lives.

Twentieth verse: "For if our heart condemn us, God is greater than our heart, and knoweth all things." Sometimes when we try to do good something seems to go wrong. We feel we have failed, and it worries us. God understands our hearts and He knows our motives.

Twenty-first verse: "Beloved, if our heart condemn us not, then have we confidence toward God." Happy is the man or woman with a clear conscience, who can approach our Heavenly Father with joy and confidence in perfect fellowship.

Twenty-second, twenty-third and twenty-fourth verses: "And whatsoever we ask, we receive of him, because we keep his commandments, and do those things that are pleasing in his sight. And this is his commandment, That we should believe on the name of his Son Jesus Christ, and love one another, as he gave us commandment. And he that keepeth his commandments dwelleth in him, and he in him. And hereby we know that he abideth in us, by the Spirit which he hath given us." When we make our requests known to God, we can be assured that He will answer us, because Jesus said, "Seek and ye shall find," and "Ask and it shall be given you." But Jesus also said if we do not get the answer we expected, it is because we asked *amiss*. If we are in complete accordance with the will of God, instead of self-will, we will be keeping His commandments, and *doing* things that are pleasing in His sight.

God commanded us to believe on the name of His Son Jesus Christ, because on the Mount of Transfiguration, the voice of God said, "This is my beloved Son . . . hear ye him!" If we truly believe and love the Lord Jesus Christ, we will love one another, because He is in our brother as well as in us. We know that He abides in us, by His Holy Spirit, because He promised He would send the Comforter, who guides us into all truth—and Jesus is Truth.

Lovingly yours,
Mother.

Dear Tom

I hope I am not abusing your patience with these discussions of the truth I am finding in John. It isn't that I am setting myself up as a Bible scholar or expositor—it is just that I think we must all work out a philosophy of life on the basis of God's truth in the Bible. I am finding so *much* in these three little Bible letters that I just have to pass it along to you. Read them for yourself; maybe you will come up with a lot I have missed. That's the wonder of the Bible: you can read it and read it and *read* it—and the next time you read it, there is a whole new world of truth and light that you missed before.

In our last letter I discussed I John 3; today I have been reading I John 4, and here are some of my reactions.

First, second and third verses: "Beloved, believe not every spirit, but try the spirits whether they are of God: because many false prophets are gone out into the world.

Hereby know ye the Spirit of God: Every spirit that confesseth that Jesus Christ is come in the flesh is of God: And every spirit that confesseth not that Jesus Christ is come in the flesh is not of God: and this is that spirit of antichrist, whereof ye have heard that it should come; and even now already is it in the world." There are more spirits than just one—for Jesus cast a *dumb* spirit out of a man. He also cast out many evil spirits from an insane man. These particular evil spirits said their name was *Legion*, signifying many evil spirits in the one man. Today, when a person is committed to an insane asylum, he usually has many obsessions and very real fears and hates. In days of old, they said these people were *demon-possessed*. Today, we call them psychopathic, schizophrenic, etc. But no matter what the term is, the hapless victim is a victim of evil spirits. The one true Spirit is the Holy Spirit, sent from God. A true, practicing Christian will not have a mental breakdown, because his mental strength comes from God and the Holy Spirit brings peace, that peace that passes all understanding, that strange calm that is found in the center of a storm.

The first verse tells us to try the spirits whether they are of God, because many false prophets are gone out into the world. The test of the suggesting spirit is to determine if the spirit is Christian. When we are given advice, we should be careful to see if the advice is of a selfish nature, to benefit only ourselves. It is very popular today to consult a psychiatrist when everything goes wrong in life. Personally, I would look for a minister, because a real servant of God knows more real psychiatry than anyone else. Actually, mere psychiatry is a diagnosis, rarely the cure. If the psychiatrist is a Christian, he is in a wonderful position to diagnose and cure, because he will inspire the patient to have faith in Christ, to heal the diagnosed infirmities of the mind and soul.

As Mrs. Hayward so aptly pegged the term "antichrist" a few Sundays ago, the spirit of antichrist is not *yet* to come—*it is already here.* The beloved disciple, John, writes in this epistle, "and this is that spirit of antichrist, whereof ye have heard that it should come; and even now already is it in the world." Indeed, it is now in the world, in 1956, even as it was then and even as far back as Adam and Eve, for the source of antichrist is Satan himself. Satan has always been antichrist, for Satan's spiritual pride, which caused him to want to be equal with God, resulted in his being cast down from heaven to the lower realm. Satan despises humility and therefore he despised Jesus and sought to overthrow our Lord as the Messiah when he tempted Jesus in the wilderness, telling Him to command the stones to become bread, to break His holy discipline of fasting. Satan knew he was no match for our Lord in the matter of love, so he tried to trip Him through the temptation of spiritual pride. But Jesus said, "Thou shall not tempt the Lord, thy God!" Yes, antichrist means denying the Deity of Jesus Christ. If we are not *for* Christ, we are *against* Christ, or antichrist. There is no such thing as neutrality in this matter.

Fourth, fifth and sixth verses: "Ye are of God, little children, and have overcome them: because greater is he that is in you, than he that is in the world. They are of the world: therefore speak they of the world, and the world heareth them. We are of God: he that knoweth God heareth us; he that is not of God heareth not us. Hereby know we the spirit of truth, and the spirit of error." The Christians are told, "Ye are of God, little children, and have overcome them." We are likened to little children, because unless we become as little children in our faith, trusting implicitly in the Lord for our guidance, we cannot enter the kingdom of God. This is understandable, because if we lean toward our own understanding instead of committing our way unto the Lord, we will have no peace—and peace is the fruit of the Holy Spirit working for and through us. Christ in us is greater than Satan in the world. Christ ascended into heaven. Satan fell *from* heaven, and Christ in us will rise above the satanic influence in the world.

Christians recognize other Christians quickly, for they are of one mind, the mind of Christ. Non-Christians do not "hear" or understand Christians, because the one sees through the eyes of the world, which is bound and blinded by Satan, and the other sees through the eyes of Christ, with spiritual sight. The preaching of the cross is foolishness to them that perish, but to us, who are being saved by Christ, it is the power of God.

Seventh, eighth, ninth, tenth and eleventh verses: "Beloved, let us love one another: for love is of God; and every one that loveth is born of God, and knoweth God. He that loveth not knoweth not God; for God is love. In this was manifested the love of God toward us, because that God sent his only begotten Son into the world, that we might live through him. Herein is love, not that we loved God, but that he loved us, and sent his Son to be the propitiation for our sins. Beloved, if God so loved us, we ought also to love one another." We are told, as Christians, to love one another, for love is of God. If we do not love each other, we do not know God, for God is Love. If we do not love each other, we do not love God, and if we do not love God, we will not keep His commandments—and then it is blasphemy to call ourselves Christian. Think of the magnitude of God's love for us. While we were yet sinners without any love for Him, He cared enough about us to send His only begotten Son, to die on the Cross of Calvary in our place, so that we might be justified to live eternally with Him. Can you imagine sending your only child out among enemies to be killed so that the enemies will be saved? I can't—but how grateful we should be to God for such unselfish love! If He could do this for us, surely we can love each other.

Twelfth verse: "No man hath seen God at any time. If we love one another, God dwelleth in us, and his love is perfected in us." Jesus said, "God is a spirit and they that worship him shall worship him in spirit and in truth." The Scripture says if we love one another, God dwelleth in us and His love is perfected in us. *God is Love.* Now what is the definition of the word *love?* There are many, but the Apostle Paul tells us that though we speak with the tongues of men and of angels and have not charity, we are become as sounding brass, or a tinkling cymbal—in other words, our *love* is hollow.

Webster's definition of *love:* "Love is a feeling of strong personal attachment, induced by sympathetic understanding, or by ties of kinship, or affection, such as benevolence attributed to God, as being like a father's affection for his children, and also as men's adoration for God." Benevolence attributed to God—benevolence is much the same as charity. St. Paul says, "Charity suffereth long, and is kind; charity envieth not; charity vaunteth not itself, is not puffed up, Doth not behave itself unseemly, seeketh not her own, is not easily provoked, thinketh no evil; Rejoiceth not in iniquity, but rejoiceth in the truth; Beareth all things, believeth all things (all things work together for good), hopeth all things (has faith in God's wisdom), endureth all things."

Thirteenth and fourteenth verses: "Hereby know we that we dwell in him, and he in us, because he hath given us of his Spirit. And we have seen and do testify that the Father sent the Son to be the Saviour of the world." These disciples truly lived with Jesus, saw Him die, and saw Him after His resurrection. They can prove by His reappearance after death that He was really the Saviour, who came into the world to save sinners; that He is Truth and Love, and unconquerable, even by death.

Lovingly yours,
Mother.

Dear Tom

Will wonders never cease? Here we are aboard a DC-7, high over Grand Canyon—all seven children, father and I, and Mrs. Wright, our "helping hand" with the children. Ohio State Fair, here we come! Tom, I wondered many times during the past few days if we would really make it. It just shows what the strength of the Lord can do! "The Lord is my strength and my shield." Yes, indeed, He is. I started one week ago packing for the tour, and believe me, with "show clothes" and street clothes for seven children, it's no small task.

We always send our show clothes and equipment in our big trunks, in the horse van with Glenn Randall, the trainer, and Trigger, Trigger Jr., and Buttermilk. They have to be picked up a week in advance of our departure, so they will be there when we arrive by plane. All the kids' stage clothes were packed in an old-fashioned trunk that you lift by handles—they hold more!

Three days ago I started on the suitcases. The three big girls were given charts for packing, and I packed for Dusty, Sandy, Dodie, Debbie and "Mama." Mrs. Wright came over last night and we planned our early morning "get-away." At five-thirty the alarm called us, and father and I jumped out of the sack and put on the coffee and teapot for the children. They breakfasted on orange juice, toast, and hot coffee or tea, while father cooked his usual two eggs, bacon, coffee, etc. I dressed the two little girls and myself, tied the boys' ties and the big girls' Western string ties, had a spot of coffee and orange juice while Pearl Wright washed the dishes, and Danny Lock, our foreman, was loading the baggage. Danny brought the pickup truck and loaded all fifteen pieces of baggage and put the two boys in the front seat with him, and they took off to check us in at the airport. Our good friend, Jack O'Shea, drove with the rest of us in the station wagon, and we arrived at eight A.M. to meet Mike North, of the Roy Rogers company, who had our tickets. They allowed us to board the plane ahead of time with our "stock company," as someone wanted pictures taken as we boarded.

At the moment, the two little girls and father are asleep; the rest are enjoying themselves thoroughly, and I am purring almost as loudly as the DC-7, because now I can draw a deep breath again! We are due to arrive in Columbus at 7:30 P.M., where Art Rush and Al Rackin and Art's wonderful secretary and "girl Friday," Helen Young, will meet us. We have a slight layover in Chicago between planes.

Lots of folks have said to me, "You are really asking

for it, to take all seven kids on this trip." But, you know, Tom, it's easier this way, because I can put my finger on each one of them, instead of being two thousand miles away and wondering. . . .

I know we will all enjoy going to Duck Run with Roy, and having him show the children his childhood haunts. Pat Brady is with us on the plane this morning. The rest of the Pioneers will meet us for rehearsal at the hotel Wednesday evening. I think it will be fun doing my new tune, "Pioneer Woman," with the Pioneers. This little song is a tribute to our pioneer grandmothers, who really "put their shoulders to the wheel" in helping their mates conquer the West. Women today have it so easy—washing machines and dryers, permanent waves, electric stoves, running water, central heating and air conditioning. A couple of times our water pump has broken down and we have had to "tote" water. Believe me, I've a healthy respect for our pioneering women. I think we women today wouldn't have so many complexes and neuroses and various chronic ailments if we had to function as those hardy souls did! It makes one a little ashamed, when one compares the living conditions of the two eras. Of course, I suppose the mortality rate in childbirth was higher, but I'll bet if the figures were really known we'd find that the babies were healthier and had more real sense of security from birth, because a woman in those days thought more about her child than she did about keeping her own figure a "perfect thirty-six." Not that I think it's wrong for a woman to want to look nice—but what's the point in half starving during pregnancy, when there are actually two mouths to feed instead of one? I think our grandmothers were wise when they "thought good" and "ate good" during pregnancy. How did I ever get off on this stream of thought?

So glad you and Barbara and my grandbabies, Mindy and Candy, are having a wonderful vacation up in Yreka. Yes, I can understand why you prefer the high mountain country to living in crowded Los Angeles. Los Angeles is a fine city and I love it, but traffic is terrible and so is the smog. How grateful I am that the smog hasn't yet reached Chatsworth. Occasionally it sneaks in, but for the most part our ranch is clear and shining.

Last week, while talking to Margie Hamilton, little Nancy's mother, she said since Nancy's death the bookstores can't keep abreast of the orders for *Red Shoes for Nancy*. Isn't that wonderful? You see, through Christ, Nancy has indeed triumphed over the grave—for she is alive in so many seeking hearts through the printed word of her own story. Margie showed me stacks of mail from all over the world, and since the news of her death, her desk is constantly flooded. What a blessed and active comfort for Margie in ministering to Nancy's friends from all corners. She said each time a wave of human grief for Nancy hits her, she gets a fresh batch of letters from those who need spiritual help badly; and then she realizes she hasn't the time for the "luxury" of pining for Nancy. It's as if Nancy said, "Okay, Mom, knock it off and get to my work—time's a-wasting!" Incredible soul, that Margie Hamilton, and altogether lovely. The Lord did a handsome piece of modeling through His blessed little instrument who had but one real material desire—a pair of red shoes, which she was never to wear. Like Robin, wings more become her.

I just opened my Bible to the Eighteenth Psalm of David. Isn't that a revealing message? It reminds me of the "pep talk" I had with the children last night, about behaving themselves at the table. Marion and Dusty cannot seem to refrain from teasing each other, and very often it gets a "bit acid" for the dinner table. A younger brother can be extremely trying, if one is inclined to look for mischief in him! Dusty has only to smirk in her direction, and they're off! Cheryl used to be his sparring partner, but she seems to be outgrowing it. I sit between Dodie and Debbie, so there's no confusion there. Father decided he would sit between Marion and Dusty, and relieve the "strain" on both of them!

The Psalm says, "With the merciful thou wilt shew thyself merciful; with an upright man thou wilt shew thyself upright; With the pure thou wilt shew thyself pure; and with the *froward* thou wilt shew thyself froward." Does this not mean that we should be careful of what *type* of bread we cast upon the waters? If we cast sour bread, we're certain to get sour dough back. If we cast sweet morsels, they will be sweet in return. Actually, the children all love each other, and they are like any other bunch of brothers and sisters, scrapping one minute and loving the next. It hardly behooves a parent to get agitated over the usual bickering, except that I believe every family table is the Lord's table, and mealtime should be a time of blessed enjoyment, spiritually as well as physically, because the Lord is our unseen Member, and I dare say He does not enjoy confusion—since the devil is the author of it!

You know, as we are smoothly and swiftly airborne toward Chicago, it is very assuring to know that this plane and all the occupants are held "in the hollow of His hand." The Bible says it is impossible to go anywhere where God is not, because He fills all. Why should we fret about an accident over which we would have no control? It is more important that we learn to number our days so that we may apply our hearts to wisdom and be ready when our summonses come.

Lovingly yours,
Mother.

Dear Tom

Here it is September second, Sunday evening, and our Ohio and Iowa State Fair engagements are completed. The bags are all packed, and we leave Des Moines tomorrow at noon for California and the Double R Bar Ranch in Chatsworth!

Tom, these past two weeks have been wonderful. You know, two months ago I wondered just how this family of mine would survive this two-week state fair safari, but the Lord has handled it beautifully! I know He was the One who made things go so smoothly, because I told Him that I couldn't possibly "hold together" unless He took over. Every time I secretly drifted into any apprehension about taking all seven children, I just said, "Lord, I know You will supply the strength and wisdom for Roy, the children, Pearl Wright and me to do all these shows to Your glory and take us home again." We have only had one case of sickness: Sandy overate on the plane coming to Des Moines from

Columbus. He paid for it the night we arrived here at the hotel! The food trays on the plane (which was slightly bumpy) looked so inviting that Sandy had two or three helpings—carbonated water and a short "fast" straightened him out!

The night before we opened in Columbus there was a terrific rainstorm. We couldn't even have a dress rehearsal because our show was outdoors! We "hit the show" cold on the matinee next afternoon, and everything went off like clockwork! Again, we just said a prayer for the Lord to "perfect that which concerned us." The children, all of them, performed like veterans. It was a wonderful feeling, giving a Christian witness as a family unit to so many other family units sitting in the grandstands. Dodie sang a "condensed version" of "Jesus Loves Me," and Debbie sang "Tula-lula-lula" (Tura-lura-lura!). Roy explained that this was the lullaby song the older girls and I sing to Dodie and Debbie at bedtime. When Dodie's unabashed childish treble produced the strains of "Jesus Loves Me," I thought what a pity that so many of us grow up embarrassed and fearful of talking and singing about the One who loves us the most! How I pray she will never question His love for her.

We all went to Duck Run, Ohio, and to Portsmouth, to see Roy's "childhood haunts." I think that was a real thrill for Roy, to show the children the home of his childhood—and a pretty home it was! The rolling hills, so verdant with summer foliage, and the friendly farmhouses were very gracious in welcome. We went to the little church, to the country store, and to the house that

Roy and his father built. The people there are "folksy" and comfortable to have around. We enjoyed going into the house and seeing the changes that have been made by Mrs. Hiles, the present occupant and a long-time friend of Roy's folks. We also stopped in Portsmouth to see the little houseboat that Roy played in, the first year or so of his life. His Uncle Bill, who is blind, lives there still, doing his own housework, cooking, etc., among friendly neighbors. Uncle Bill has the face of a saint, as blind people so often do. He sees nothing ugly. When Roy introduced Dodie, our little Indian maid, to Uncle Bill, he fondled her long, dark and silky hair, and saw her through the touch of his gentle hands. His face lighted up like a Christmas tree! One of the children asked Roy how he became blind, and Roy explained how Uncle Bill and another boy were throwing sand at each other. The other boy threw a handful in Uncle Bill's eyes—only it wasn't just sand, but contained tiny pieces of broken glass. To this day, Roy has a fit when he sees kids throwing dirt in each other's faces.

We made our visit to the Portsmouth and Duck Run area the day after arriving in Columbus. Business was excellent and it didn't "rain us out" once, praise the Lord!

On Sunday, the twenty-sixth, we all went to Trinity Episcopal Church, three blocks from the hotel, and heard an excellent sermon on being a good soldier of Jesus Christ. I enjoyed it so much. However, as I glanced at the date on the service folder, there was a twinge of nostalgia, for it was my angel's birthday. Then I remembered that we have communion with the saints, and that we are encompassed by a cloud of witnesses, and my Robin was right there in the pew for her birthday. There were flowers sent to the crypt at Forest Lawn, but the real flowers were from my spirit to hers. Blessed Christian assurance! Would to our Blessed Lord that every despairing mother in the world had it!

On Monday before we left Columbus, Roy and I visited a fifteen-year-old boy at University Hospital. His name was Ronnie Stonerock, and he was just about through with his fight with leukemia. It isn't often that I fall apart at the seams after one of these visits, because I realize that we are on tour to entertain and help others, and you can't do it with a tearful face. This blessed boy undid me, though. The experience was very humbling because we were privileged to see a remarkable example of Christian courage. Ronnie, his mother explained, is a Christian, and he was interested in us primarily because of our Christian faith. To visit with us was one of his last requests. I couldn't see how the boy could still be alive when we first saw him—he was in an oxygen tent and his spirit seemed to be struggling for freedom. However, he came out of that oxygen tent to have his picture made with us (one of his requests). He could barely speak, because of his labored breathing, but his eyes said everything. The nurse in attendance said he had been a blessing to everyone in the hospital, because of his courage and faith in Jesus. In weakness is Christ made strong! We had prayer with him, his mother and his sister—a prayer of thanksgiving for the Reality of Christ and the privilege of spending eternity in His presence. . . . There was no fear on Ronnie's face. He knew he was on his way to a better future!

On the way out, we visited other leukemia patients, some teen-age and some very young. The tiny boys and girls were still able to say to Roy, "Stick 'em up!" although I saw many telltale bruises on young white skin, and with a pang of sadness realized that their days were numbered. Many ask, "Why, why? These little ones haven't had a chance to bloom in the garden of life!" Well, Tom, God is the Gardener, and if He wants a lovely bud to grace His Home, isn't it His privilege to pluck it? Who knows what tragedy that little boy or girl might have experienced later in this reeling universe? We know they are safe with our Lord, because He said, "Of such is the kingdom of heaven."

The Iowa State Fair has been very enjoyable, too. We did our last matinee yesterday afternoon. This morning we went to church at the First Methodist Church and heard a very inspiring and challenging message, "On the Job," by Reverend Wilbur Wilcox. It seemed as if it were custom-tailored for us, because it had to do with serving the Lord in your job, whatever the job is. That minister faces right up to the issue of "Can a Christian be a good Christian in work outside of full-time Christian work, such as missionary effort, preaching, teaching, etc.?" Of course, he said, if a job is definitely contrary to Christian principle and demoralizing to society, and one honestly feels that way about it, one should give up that job. In other words, that man or woman's heart would so condemn and convict him of aiding the adversary that he would be practically *forced* to give up the job, or lose his Christian peace. He told the story of a Scottish Presbyterian minister who sat next to a humble little man on the train and asked him what he did for the Lord. The little man quietly replied, "I bake bread." Like Brother Lawrence, who constantly practiced the presence of God while performing his daily kitchen tasks, this little man baked bread to the glory of God the Father, the Son, and the Holy Ghost. Since bread is called "the staff of life," and is certainly symbolic of the True Bread from Heaven, Christ our Lord, this little man had quite a vocation!

Lovingly yours,
Mother.

Dear Tom

It's September and back to school. . . . I so enjoyed talking to your little Mindy on the telephone last evening about her first day at kindergarten.

I am writing this aboard an American Air Lines non-stop liner to New York, to attend our annual luncheon with the licensees of Roy Rogers' and Dale Evans' merchandise during the fall showings for buyers. We will spend just one day in New York and then head back for home, because I want to get back in time to rearrange our "shooting schedule" for school and home routine.

After returning home from the State Fairs, we gave the three oldest girls a reasonable amount of money to do their September school shopping for clothes. This time I didn't go with them. I told them to go over their wardrobes carefully and shop accordingly. You know, we were very pleased at their prudence and taste! Each one had money left over, and each girl was quite thrilled with her accomplishment. They *have* to like these clothes because they chose them! It certainly saves "Mama" a lot of wear and tear, and it spares her remarks like, "*Nobody* wears that!" It is very hard for mothers to realize that their teen-age daughters are capable of selecting a wardrobe alone. For me, it was like pulling eye teeth, for I enjoyed choosing things for them myself! However, the girls convinced me yesterday that they are growing up, at least in this matter.

School is a wonderful institution, Tom. I never quite realized until this summer just how much security school gives to a child. A child feels secure in a definite program. Several times this summer our children remarked, "I'll be glad when school starts. There's nothing to do!" Nothing to do—with a swimming pool, horses, bikes, television, mountains to climb, books to read, and any number of projects they could start! A definite program makes the difference. Come next summer, the Lord willing, I am going to launch a summer program, with a time schedule, so they won't feel "too free with nothing to do." To me, this is just further proof that every human needs a program, in order to avoid the pitfall of frustration.

I was so thrilled yesterday with Dr. Lucius Lindley's report of progress made by his group of retarded children. He was one of the very first doctors to believe that these little youngsters *can* be helped. He, along with the Clinic for Mental Retardation at Children's Hospital in Los Angeles, is providing a *program* for these youngsters; and that, combined with the love, faith, and cooperation of their parents, is paying off. One little three-year-old is attending regular nursery school, and filling her place in that school nicely. I just couldn't stop the tears when he told me. What I would have given for little Robin to attend regular nursery school! However, she accomplished more by her early graduation from this life. Had she gone on living, she might not have been able to speak in such a far-reaching way. She must be very happy for her little "fellow missionaries" who are, and will be, finding better and better working conditions.

Back to your little Mindy and her elation over kindergarten: Wouldn't it be wonderful if humans could always get a thrill out of learning in the school of life? If we could approach each trial, lesson, or pleasure with the anticipation of "What can I learn from this?" Instead, we recoil with fear. This means we are shrinking from the love of God, because the Bible says, "Perfect love casteth out fear." Oh, that we would emblazon this Scripture on our hearts with indelible faith, backed by the sure promises of our Lord Jesus Christ!

Wisdom! The Bible tells us to get wisdom—and where is wisdom to be found? Proverbs 2:6 says, "For the Lord giveth wisdom: out of his mouth cometh knowledge and understanding." In verses ten and eleven we read: "When wisdom entereth into thine heart, and knowledge is pleasant unto thy soul; Discretion shall preserve thee, understanding shall keep thee." How wonderful it is to have the privilege of *learning*. If we could just impress that upon our children—yes, and on ourselves—perhaps the newspapers would read a little differently on the subject of crime among teen-agers *and* adults! The Bible is, to me, the supreme source of learning for a fruitful life. There are so many fine systems of

Bible study for family groups that I am going to search thoroughly for one that each member of our family can appreciate. It should be interesting to our four-year-olds, nine-year-olds, and teen-agers—as well as to "Pops" (as Dusty and Sandy call their Daddy) and to me. Family projects should serve each member of the family, and I believe a corporate enjoyment of the Bible by the family is vitally important in family and outside relations.

A letter came this week from a distressed mother of adopted children, who had rather dark skins and who had already received a bit of nasty discrimination from an outsider. God bless her for housing these little war orphans, and protect her home with a formidable fortress of Christian love and understanding! God created us all, and He has never created any two beings exactly alike, nor did He create the races alike as to color. Who can know the mind of God? Who can say which color is best in His eyes? Christ lived and died for all, regardless of race, creed, or color. How long will we wallow in this quicksand of racial intolerance?

The Book of Acts, in the New Testament, tells the story of Philip baptizing an Ethiopian eunuch, a person of great authority under Candace, Queen of the Ethiopians, having charge of all her treasure and who had come to Jerusalem to worship. Philip explained the Scriptures concerning Jesus, and baptized this seeking Ethiopian. The Bible says they *both* went down into the water, and Philip baptized him. Philip was Greek, and a man very busy ministering to his own people; but, constrained by his love for Christ, he made the friendly overture to the man of the different race, with no regard for possible rebuff, or for difference in color, race, or custom.

Teaching of racial tolerance must begin in the home. These little adopted children of different racial backgrounds must have a home that is solid in love and understanding; their little feet must be shod very early with the Gospel of our Lord Jesus Christ, and their armour must be securely linked with the profound truths of our God, who is a God of love and mercy, as well as of justice. If the child is "well steeped" in Christian upbringing, he will be able to withstand the cruel and foolish darts of the unlearned.

The other night, from the recently bereaved parents of an angelically beautiful little girl of eight, I heard the pitiful story of a formerly respected man, who, apparently at the suggestion of Satan, kidnapped and murdered their child. Someone gave them a copy of *Angel Unaware*, and they came to Los Angeles, visited little Robin's crypt at Forest Lawn, and then came to see Roy and me at the ranch. In spite of the blinding anguish just ahead of having to face this man and relive this tragedy throughout his trial, I saw the Light of Christ and the "peace which passeth all understanding" on their faces. They said, "When we were knocked to our knees by this blow, there was only one way to look—up!" And the father said they have been looking up toward the Lord ever since. However, the tragedy has a happy issue in the sealed faith of the parents and a new children's wing in their city hospital, built by compassionate townspeople as a memorial to this little angel. We had prayer together, and we prayed the forgiveness of God for this man, who was once some mother's adored "little one," and who, somehow, lost his way and heeded the tempter.

Well, we're high in the clouds, speeding back toward California. This was a quick but very enjoyable trip. The "fall showing" of our merchandise to prospective buyers was very attractively handled. You might say it was a "merchandise roundup," with luncheon chuck-wagon style! We visited our manufacturers, and also the buyers. You know, Tom, it is very exciting to have your "brand" on something for children, and it is also quite a responsibility. Therefore, we feel it necessary to keep close to the merchandise situation, because a shoddy piece of merchandise reflects on what we stand for, in the same way as a backsliding Christian is a reflection on (not of) Christianity. Some people may say that actors endorse products simply for monetary gain, but that is not always true. Some actors believe in their products as a service to the public, as well as enjoying the royalties derived therefrom. It is particularly satisfying to endorse a product that will make a child's face glow with pleasure. This is a real privilege and should not be taken lightly.

Roy and I just finished reading the autobiography of Henry Armstrong, the colored boxing star. This is one of the greatest and most challenging stories I have ever read! Every American should read the last chapter, and reflect on what America stands for. God bless Henry Armstrong and those like him who are waging a clean fight for the oppressed of our nation. No race of the human family should abide "in the shadows" in the

United States of America. Tom, I pray that the people of our land will pray before they vote in the coming election. Then may we pray that the elected President will allow God to make his decisions. There are rumors of war again rumbling, but our God is sufficient, even unto death. May we trust Him, individually and collectively.

I just noticed in a New York evening newspaper that New York City heads the nation in coronary heart disease. This is not surprising! As we sauntered along Fifth Avenue to my brother's office, I scanned the faces of the oncoming pedestrians. Very few are serene. People walk fast, drive fast, eat fast, sleep fast, think fast, work fast, play fast—and die fast. It's wonderful to see the open church doors, where the hurry-harried people may quietly slip in and cast their burdens upon Him, who can and will give peace and rest in the midst of all this teeming activity. God is so good to send the pigeons to big city parks, for they are quieting and like a benediction to the many who go there for relaxation. The people feed the birds and the birds feed the people—it's a two-way blessing!

I have received several letters from parents who, through mitigating circumstances, had to place their retarded children in institutions. They feel that something should be written to comfort the hearts of those parents who could not keep their children at home. I have never meant to sit in judgment on these unfortunate parents. I meant to imply that I believed it better, if possible, to keep the child at home, to join a parents' council for the retarded, to find a sympathetic physician, and to go on from there. If parents are unable to do this, then the main thing, I believe, is that they keep loving the child and visiting him regularly, never resorting to the final and helpless feeling that the child is a "lost cause" and forever shut off from life. One of the most rewarding things parents can do is to have a "program" for the child. In other words, keep trying, through study of mental retardation, and helping and encouraging the caretakers of the child on the regular visits. It is terribly frustrating to resign yourself to the thought that "nothing can be done." Usually much can be done to improve the situation. The Bible says, "I can do all things through Christ, Who strengtheneth me"; and "Have faith, hope, and charity (love)." Faith *believes*, hope does not give up, charity *serves*.

Lovingly yours,
Mother.

Dear Tom

Another plane flight to Dallas, to pick up Mom and bring her back to Chatsworth to stay for a while. (I wish I could persuade her to stay permanently!) She hasn't been feeling too well, and I want her near, where I can do a little "nursing." Always I shall be grateful to my Mom for her loving concern and care of you, my brother and me, when we were all young. There was a time when she didn't have her clothes off for three days and nights, as she applied ice packs behind your ear to circumvent a dangerous mastoid operation. The specialist let Mom try it, even though he held no hope for reducing the swelling. But our Mom had faith in the Lord and in her ice therapy—and the swelling finally went down. Shortly afterward your tonsils were removed and that was the end of the mastoid trouble. "Son," my brother, was in school; I was working as a stenographer, and we had two boarders at the house. Mom managed, bless her, to keep it all going. Then there was her wonderful nursing through the three months I spent in bed during my nervous breakdown when I was eleven.

Children in our country are so prone to take these things for granted, but it is not so among other peoples, where parents are respected and cherished with gratitude for their sacrifices in behalf of the child. As a Christian nation, we parents and children should heed the commandment, "Honour thy father and thy mother: that thy days may be long . . ."—that thy days may be *long*, and, I believe, happy! There is joy in "doing" for our parents, as there is joy in doing for our children.

Ought our aged years not be made happy with the confidence that those whom we have carefully nurtured and loved unselfishly will return it to us, as we become more dependent in the dusk of life? In Oriental culture, age is respected and honored. It seems to me they understand this commandment of filial obligation better than we do. Shame on us, for feeling that age is a blight! As trees become more beautiful with age, so should a human being! I believe we have a false concept of age, due to our looking at it from the negative viewpoint of deterioration rather than development. Only in America, it seems, is youth put on a pedestal and worshiped. Why can't we grow old graciously, as well as gracefully? Why should we shudder at the first silver streaks in our hair? Why do we fight wrinkles with every device known to man (and woman!), spending extravagant sums of money and time to keep a baby-smooth skin, when we should be spending that time in ironing out the wrinkles in our natures? Yes, Tom, my hair is "silvering" rapidly, and has been for quite a while. Let it! I do not spend money on face creams and hair dyes! Why wear yourself out fighting the inevitable, when there is so much to enjoy in the present? All we have is the present—the past is gone, and the future belongs to God. I want to keep fit mentally and physically, and by the grace of God to be about my Father's business of performing the task at hand to His glory.

I have been asked, "What is the secret of your youthful appearance?" If I do appear younger than my actual age, the answer is no secret: I don't worry about growing old. There is not enough time to indulge in such fruitless nonsense. "For as he thinketh in his heart, so is he. . . ." We can fear age and look old, or we can enjoy maturing, and look young. It is the attitude that counts. God keeps me young. I never intend to grow old, if I live to be a hundred. In the first place, the minute Jesus Christ invaded my heart, new life coursed through my veins. He gave and still gives me life, abundant—zestful, interesting, stimulating. The idea, I have found, is to let Him live in you, and when that happens, there is constant unfolding, a reaching outward, instead of that clutching inward which shrivels the body and the personality.

Lovingly yours,
Mother.

Dear Tom

Roy is on a plane bound for Africa, no less! He is going on a safari to hunt big game. Honestly, he reminded me of the kids at Christmastime, when he was showing off his beautiful new gun, first-aid kit, and the little tape recorder on which he will narrate the exciting events, the narration fitting the action film as it is taken daily. He has long wanted to go on a big game hunt, and I am so glad he could! The children and I will meet him in New York on November twentieth, just before the day of the Macy's parade, in which we all participate. Hope we have real chilly weather, and maybe snow, because the children would really enjoy some bona fide winter weather! California is a wonderful place to live, but I do miss the definite seasons of the year when winter is winter, spring is spring, summer is summer, and fall is fall!

I was just reading the Ninetieth Psalm and came upon the wonderful passage: "So teach us to number our days, that we may apply our hearts unto wisdom," and a New Testament scripture from Ephesians (5:16) flashed before me: "Redeeming the time, because the days are evil." Yes, there is much evil abroad today. Satan is attacking us in a below-the-belt manner, through our children. He is certainly walking about as a roaring lion, seeking whom he may devour. This week there have been two knife slayings of young women in two days, in the same town. A seventeen-year-old boy confessed to one of them and admitted he had taken a "pop" of heroin earlier that morning.

Yes, the days are evil, but we can redeem the time by applying our hearts to the Word of God, the Bible, and prayer, and living the Christian life before the coming generation. We parents needn't think the churches and schools can handle *all* the molding of our children. They say a schoolteacher can tell a lot about the home life a child has, without even meeting the parents, by the child's attitude and behavior! We cannot say, "Don't do as I do, do as I say." We must *do* as we want them to do, if they are to do it.

Our country heads the list in untimely heart disease —what a sad commentary. Where do we think we are going in such a hurry? If we adults don't simmer down, how can our children be calm and deliberate in their decisions? How can we calm down? By stopping dead-still in the midst of confusion, and remembering that "The earth is the Lord's and all that therein is"—and remembering also that God is *not* the author of confusion. When we allow ourselves to get all jittery, Satan is exultant, because then we make rash and wrong decisions. I am preaching to myself now, Tom, and I had better be listening, because there are seven young ones watching constantly to see if I practice what I preach. When I don't, which is often, I apologize to them and to God—because a child must have honesty in his parents, if he is to be honest with others and himself.

Roy and I had the pleasure of lunching with Mr. Bill Power, of the Chevrolet Company, last week. He is a most extraordinary man, and a delightfully refreshing one, in these jaded days. This man was in Y.M.C.A. work before he joined the Chevrolet Company. He is an everyday practicing Christian in his life and work. He gave the credit for his remarkable life of faith to his mother, who was left a widow with a dozen children, and no money. He said his mother was the greatest "salesman" he ever knew. In counseling the boys about their future, she said, "You can be a successful man and smoke or drink, but you can be a greater man if you don't!" This wasn't the exact quotation, but the essence of it. He has never smoked nor drunk, and is an extremely successful, respected, and happy man. His countenance is simply radiant with his love of Christ and his fellow man. He addresses youth groups and businessmen's groups constantly, in addition to his fine work with his company, and the man has boundless energy. This, to my way of thinking, is success with a capital "S." He should write a book! He likens a business organization to the church of our Lord Jesus Christ. He says it starts with one man, and branches out—and that the biblical account of the appointment of Christ's disciples and followers is the most accurate and dependable guide for running an organization. The early church had its Board of Directors, a man put over each territory, and a trouble-shooter (like St. Paul) visiting the territories regularly, admonishing, praising, suggesting, and re-capping the progress. I would love to hear him give that talk some time. He, like many other successful businessmen, has found that Jesus' way is the best and most efficient.

If Mom feels well enough, I am going to have her accompany me to Chicago for the National Safety Convention on the twenty-second of this month (October). Have to "pinch hit" for Roy, representing our interest in the school safety award. Last Saturday night we gave a Christian testimony at a huge Youth Roundup in Van Nuys. Speaking of safety, this came to me in talking to the teen-agers about safety: Being safe is not being a "square." Playing it safe is really playing it "cool," because playing it "crazy" (unsafe, in this sense) is getting in hot water—and there is nothing "cool" about that. Figures show that more children were killed by accidents this year than by the ten major diseases combined. The amazing part of it is that, according to analysis, there are more accidents in the group between the ages of nineteen and twenty-five than in the ranks of teen-agers. However, the time to ingrain "safety reflex actions" is when the child is young, by observing the rules before them ourselves, in small matters as well as in traffic crises. Doing the safe thing must come almost unconsciously, if we are really to improve our safety record. We should try somehow to show our children that being on the safe side is more fun in the long run, because we don't lose valuable time by having to "pick up the pieces" from accidents, thus allowing more time for constructive things that are fun. The word "safe" should mean achievement of security to a child, not dull restraint but something he is "smart" about. I have noticed the pride in Dusty's face when he has told me how he removed some glass that might puncture my tire, or made some toy safe for the little girls, particularly when it was his own idea. When showing a child what "not to do," we should be careful also to show him what "to do" in the same circumstance, and to show him why the right thing is superior and necessary to his well-being. This gives him a feeling of achievement in choosing the right, safe way, rather than just a feeling of being restrained.

Being on the safe side! Being on *God's* side! That's the most desirable thing in life, Tom; I'm sure of that. I'm also sure that we put ourselves there only when we obey God and submit our wills to His. The Lord Jesus Christ gave us two great commandments: "Thou shalt love the Lord thy God with all thy heart, with all thy soul, and with all thy mind. . . . And the second is like unto it, thou shalt love thy neighbour as thyself." If we concentrate on obeying these two commandments, we will be more concerned about the wonderful "Do's" in Christianity, and the "Don'ts" will fall in their proper, unimportant places in our lives. Christianity is positive and powerful. Let us be about our Father's business of doing good; let us criticize less, and pray more.

Lovingly yours,
Mother.